W9-BRH-938

Also by Craig Claiborne

The New York Times Cook Book (1961)
An Herb and Spice Cook Book (1963)
The New York Times Menu Cook Book (1966)
The New York Times Guide to Dining Out in New York (1968)

CRAIG CLAIBORNE'S
KITCHEN PRIMER

Craig Claiborne's
KITCHEN
Primer

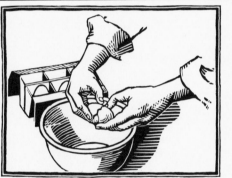

How to Crack Eggs & Other Practical Demonstrations

A basic cookbook THAT LEADS THE BEGINNER FROM HERE TO THERE IN THE KITCHEN . . . WITH ILLUSTRATIONS TO SHOW ESSENTIAL EQUIPMENT AND TECHNIQUES . . . HAVING RECIPES THROUGHOUT THAT PUT INTO PRACTICE THE FUNDAMENTALS OF GOOD COOKERY ILLUSTRATIONS BY TOM FUNK

PUBLISHED BY *ALFRED A. KNOPF* in New York MCMLXIX

THIS IS A BORZOI BOOK, PUBLISHED BY ALFRED A. KNOPF, INC.

PUBLISHED OCTOBER 15, 1969
SECOND PRINTING, OCTOBER 1969

Library of Congress Catalog Card Number: 68–23951

Manufactured in the United States of America

For Jacques, Claudia, and Diane
. . . and Velma

CONTENTS

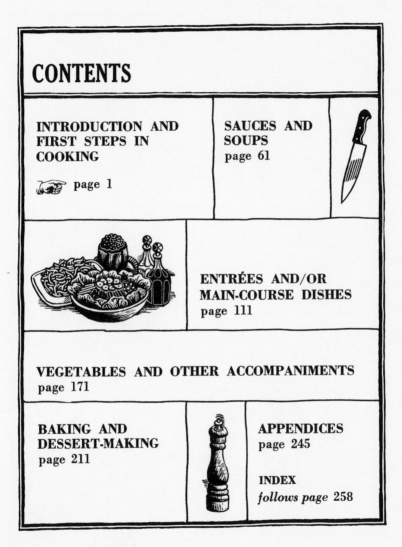

INTRODUCTION AND FIRST STEPS IN COOKING

ESSENTIAL EQUIPMENT FOR KITCHENS . . . TIPS ON PROPER USE OF EQUIPMENT, ON NEATNESS, ON ORGANIZATION . . . THE ABC's OF WEIGHTS AND MEASURES . . . THE FUNDAMENTAL TECHNIQUES OF PREPARING VEGETABLES AND FRUITS . . . A DISCOURSE ON HERBS AND SPICES . . . THE MIRACLE OF THE EGG AND ITS MULTIPLE USES, FROM BOILED EGGS TO SOUFFLÉS

FOR THOSE WHO LOVE IT, cooking is at once child's play and adult joy. And cooking done with care is an act of love.

The approach to any task or pastime is a point of view, and playing golf or boating can be a chore and bore if one is not disposed to such pleasures. But cooking is a field in which familiarity does not breed contempt. Far from it. An intimate knowledge of how to get from here to there in the kitchen makes cooking all the more worthwhile, and that is the purpose of this small volume.

Man is born to eat and in that sense it may be said that I have been involved in food for all my forty years and five. But it seems that my interest as a professional honestly came about as a child when I became involved with the wonder that heat produces on an egg, be it boiled or fried. I can even now be fascinated by merely watching water boil, and almost compulsively I love to stir a stew to see that it doesn't stick or burn. The changing of color of a roast as it turns on a spit is a thing of endless wonder, enticing as a sunset. And this is part of the joy that I would willingly communicate to anyone who wishes to cook well.

First off, I would say that the most important thing in learning to cook well and with love is a sense of organization. Ideally, all the ingredients for any single dish should be washed and trimmed, chopped, diced, or whatever before the cooking begins.

Having a pot boil over while one is rushing to chop an onion or separate the yolk from the white of an .egg is a frustrating experience. With organization, such pitfalls can be avoided.

For pleasure, one must cook with leisure, having time to ponder each act. Without organization, chaos in the kitchen becomes a phoenix too frequent. Some recipes call for butter at room temperature. So retrieve the butter from the refrigerator in time. Almost all recipes involving an oven call for preheating same. Preheat.

One of the problems that seems to plague beginners in the kitchen is a sense of insecurity, and it stems from two things. The first is improper equipment or lack of equipment in the kitchen, and this is an inhibiting thing, to say the least.

Preferably, the home kitchen should have a complete battery of substantial cooking utensils, including pots, pans, and skillets designed more for utility than beauty (most manufacturers have it the other way around), graduated sets of sharp knives from ham slicer to paring knife, an assortment of wooden spoons, and sure-footed chopping blocks. I have tried to devise a list, based on my own experience, of essentials for a small kitchen with additions for a larger, better-equipped kitchen (see pages 6–12). Spices should by all means include the basic ten—thyme, bay leaves, cayenne pepper, basil, cumin, rosemary, saffron, dry mustard, oregano, and tarragon. For a start, that will do, with the assumption that fresh parsley may always be bought—or grown in your garden or on your window sill.

The second *bête noire* for the beginning cook is a lack of daring and a fear of failure. Be assured on one point: there is much more latitude in cooking than most people believe. Let us put it this way. It is quite possible to make a not only acceptable but admirable tomato sauce with butter, onions, a few tomatoes, salt, and pepper. The same tomato sauce may be improved with a touch of thyme, a bit of parsley, and a suggestion of garlic. The sauce may be made more elaborate with the addition of mushrooms or meat, or made more exotic with the addition of a pinch of curry or oregano. The sauce may simmer for five minutes or an hour (over very low heat). The point is that a perfectly serviceable tomato sauce can be made by cooking together for five minutes a combination of butter, onion, a few tomatoes, salt, and pepper.

The fearful beginning cook must overcome the notion that there are endless critical points in every recipe. In most recipes there are encouragingly few pitfalls. One mustn't go berserk with the thought, but a quarter cup of liquid, a tablespoon more or less of butter, five minutes or so of cooking time are all variable and the sooner the beginning cook learns it the better the food will be.

Even that holy of holies, the soufflé, despite all warnings to the contrary, is not at the mercy of a split-second chronometer. Some chefs remove their soufflés after twenty minutes of cooking time, others at the end of thirty and more. In my opinion, it is harder to cook spaghetti to the proper degree of doneness (most people overcook it) and get it to the table hot than to make a proper soufflé. And have courage. The best of professionals have known (and later cherish) their early disasters.

One last thing should be said about ingredients. The recipes in this book are derived primarily from French cooking, and the basis of most French cooking is butter and cream; they are called for unstintingly here and without apology. As far as I am concerned, there are no substitutes.

And finally, there is one thing to remember in all of cookery: the time to get ready is before you start.

The Most Basic Equipment for a Small BASIC Kitchen

A heavy iron or aluminum frying pan (approximately 10 inches in diameter),  a medium wire whisk, a heavy aluminum or enameled cast-iron saucepan (1½-quart capacity), a stainless-steel paring knife, a 12-inch stainless-steel chopping knife, a swivel-bladed paring knife, a metal spatula, a long two-pronged fork, a long metal kitchen spoon, a long slotted metal kitchen spoon, a set of graduated glass measuring cups (1 to 4 cups),  a stand-

ard set metal measuring spoons, a nest of mixing

bowls, a can opener, a beer-

can opener, a flour sifter, a grater with

assorted grating surfaces, a lemon squeezer,

a funnel, a medium-size strainer, a 8-inch pie

plate, a pair of kitchen tongs for turning bacon,

chops, etc., as they cook, a rotary beater,

a colander, a wooden spoon, a pair of kitchen

scissors,  a French wire salad basket,

a teakettle, a teapot, a coffeemaker

(I prefer a drip pot with disposable filter paper),

a toaster, a pastry brush, a rubber spatula

(for scraping bowl clean), a pepper mill, a kitchen

timer (unless there is one built into the stove), a dish-

draining rack, a basting syringe, an egg

slicer, a solid hardwood chopping block to fit on a

kitchen work surface, a 3-quart heavy metal

ovenproof casserole  (also called a Dutch oven), spice

rack (with a minimum of the following spices: bay leaves, thyme,

peppercorns, tarragon, cayenne pepper, nutmeg, oregano, dry

mustard, and paprika), 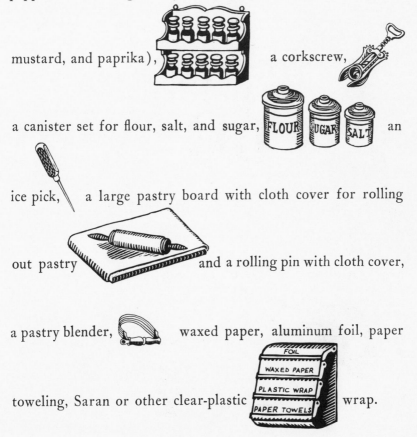 a corkscrew,

a canister set for flour, salt, and sugar, FLOUR SUGAR SALT an

ice pick, a large pastry board with cloth cover for rolling

out pastry and a rolling pin with cloth cover,

a pastry blender, waxed paper, aluminum foil, paper

toweling, Saran or other clear-plastic FOIL WAXED PAPER PLASTIC WRAP PAPER TOWELS wrap.

Additional Equipment for a
WELL-EQUIPPED Kitchen

Two more heavy iron or aluminum frying pans (8 and 12

inches in diameter), 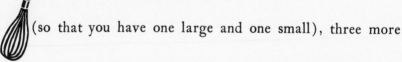 an additional wire whisk

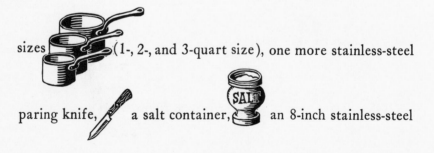 (so that you have one large and one small), three more

heavy aluminum or enameled cast-iron saucepans in graduated

sizes (1-, 2-, and 3-quart size), one more stainless-steel

paring knife, a salt container, an 8-inch stainless-steel

chopping knife, 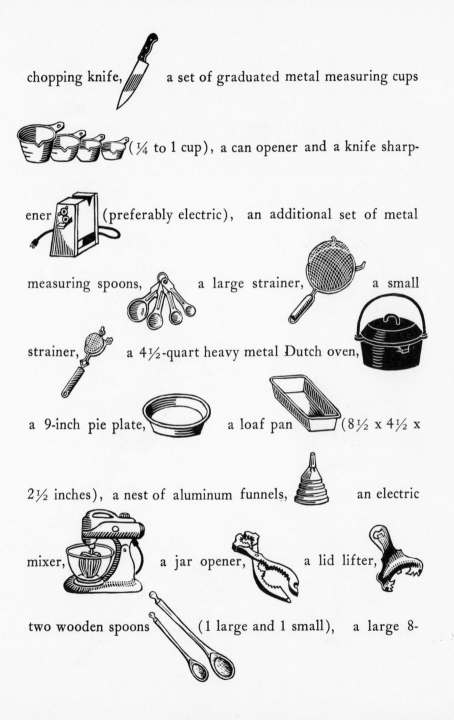 a set of graduated metal measuring cups

(¼ to 1 cup), a can opener and a knife sharp-

ener (preferably electric), an additional set of metal

measuring spoons, a large strainer, a small

strainer, a 4½-quart heavy metal Dutch oven,

a 9-inch pie plate, a loaf pan (8½ x 4½ x

2½ inches), a nest of aluminum funnels, an electric

mixer, a jar opener, a lid lifter,

two wooden spoons (1 large and 1 small), a large 8-

or 10-quart kettle for cooking soups and spaghetti,

a 2-quart soufflé dish, two or more rubber spatu-

las in different sizes, a vegetable brush, a food

mill, an electric blender, a trussing

needle and string for trussing, a large roasting

pan, a deep-fat fryer, a solid

pancake turner, a slotted pancake turner, six

custard cups, a ham slicer, a mallet for pound-

ing meat, a serrated-edge bread knife, two more

large, heavy ovenproof casseroles 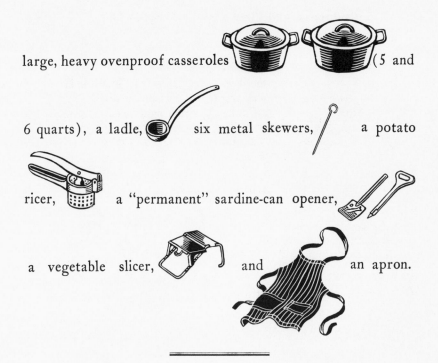 (5 and

6 quarts), a ladle, six metal skewers, a potato

ricer, a "permanent" sardine-can opener,

a vegetable slicer, and an apron.

Every kichen should have a
graduated set of mixing bowls.
Use a small bowl for mixing
small batches of foods, such as
tuna salad for two, cheese
spreads, and the like.

If you are going to whip ingredients with
a whisk or beater, think beforehand
of the expansion. Remember that egg
whites and heavy cream expand to two
or three times their original volume when
beaten. Allow room for the expansion.

Similarly, do not select bowls that are too large for practical use. When making mayonnaise, for example, remember that the beater or whisk must blend the yolks and oil rapidly, and if the bowl is too large the agitation of the two is diminished.

On Using Tongs

One of the best kitchen aids is a pair of tongs. They are far preferable to a two-pronged fork for turning meat because a fork pricks the meat and lets the juices escape. Tongs are especially useful, also, for lifting corn on the cob from a kettle of water, for lifting asparagus, and for turning bacon in a skillet.

On the Use of Knives in the Kitchen

Professional chefs almost to a man staunchly prefer knives that have carbon blades to those made of stainless steel. This is because a carbon blade will take a keener edge and, for the professional, is easy to sharpen.

For general home use, however, a set of fine stainless-steel knives is recommended for several reasons. There is the obvious reason, of course, that they do not rust or oxidize, nor do they react so quickly to acids. Onions and lemons, limes, and other citrus fruit can be sliced for hours with a stainless-steel blade without discoloration. A carbon blade, affected by oxidation or acid, will discolor the onion or fruit and will to a degree affect the flavor.

☞ *But remember,* whatever kind of kind of knife you use, it should be kept sharpened either by taking it to a professional knife grinder or sharpening it at home with a "sharpening steel" or an electric knife shapener. A dull knife is frequently more dangerous in the hands of a cook than a sharp one.

How to Keep a Kitchen Neat

Always line a working surface or a kitchen sink with waxed paper before peeling or paring vegetables, fruit, or berries.

When the peeling and paring is done, gather up the paper with the refuse and discard it.

An Apron Is a Kitchen Aid

Along with sharp knives, chopping blocks, and mixing bowls, there is an item that I rank as essential: this is the kitchen apron. It is a safeguard against a multitude of nuisances, including water sprays and spattering fats, and no professional chef would work without one.

The best aprons are those that hang around the neck or, for the ladies, perhaps smocks. The things with frills called hostess aprons are strictly for show, and if you want to wear one of those gimmicky items printed all over with coy phrases like "Chief Cook" that's all right, too, as long as it covers you.

THE MOST IMPORTANT MEASUREMENTS TO KNOW ARE THESE:

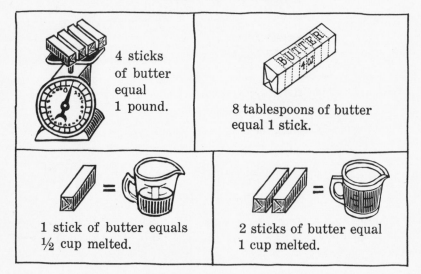

4 sticks of butter equal 1 pound.

8 tablespoons of butter equal 1 stick.

1 stick of butter equals ½ cup melted.

2 sticks of butter equal 1 cup melted.

4 tablespoons of ingredients, liquid or solid, equal ¼ cup. Therefore, 8 tablespoons of an ingredient equal ½ cup.

There are 3 teaspoons to 1 tablespoon.

1 cup equals ½ pint.

2 cups equal 1 pint.

4 cups equal 1 quart.

When measuring liquid ingredients, it is generally best to use a glass measuring cup, which can be raised to eye level to make sure the measurement is accurate.

FLO

When measuring solid ingredients, it is generally best to use metal measuring spoons or cups, which you fill to overflowing and then level off with a spatula or knife to get an exact measurement.

THE MOST USUAL WEIGHTS AND MEASURES

A pinch	=	⅛ teaspoon or less
1 tablespoon	=	3 teaspoons
4 tablespoons	=	¼ cup
8 tablespoons	=	½ cup
12 tablespoons	=	¾ cup
1 cup of liquid	=	½ pint
2 cups of liquid	=	1 pint
4 cups of liquid	=	1 quart
2 pints of liquid	=	1 quart
4 quarts	=	1 gallon
8 quarts	=	1 peck, such as apples, pears, etc.
16 ounces	=	1 pound

On Measuring Ingredients

It is always best for the novice cook to measure ingredients exactly until the "feel" of cooking is obtained. An experienced cook knows, however, that measurements down to the last grain of salt are not always necessary. That is to say, if a recipe for soup calls for a quart of broth, ½ cup of the broth more or less will probably not be critical; neither would a single rib of celery, ¼ cup of chopped onion, nor a whole or ½ clove of garlic.

Ingredients can and should be varied by an imaginative cook. When a recipe says "season to taste" or "salt to taste," it means precisely that. It leaves the seasoning to the palate of the cook.

But be cautious when using salt. Remember that it can always be added but never subtracted, and if you have a stock or sauce that is to be simmered for a considerable length of time it will become increasingly salty to the taste as the liquid cooks. Caution is particularly important in the making of beef or chicken stock, because it is frequently desirable to reduce the liquid after the original stock is made. By reducing a stock, you have a concentration of the good flavors.

To measure solid fats such as nonliquid shortening, pack the fats into a metal measuring cup or spoon, pressing down to prevent air space. Level the fat off with a straight-edged spatula or knife. Scoop the fat into a skillet, saucepan, or whatever with a rubber spatula.

There are many dishes where the beginning cook is admonished to use his or her own judgment where measurements are concerned to gain a desired effect. For example, in making dishes with cheese, the quality and strength of cheese varies tremendously. Perhaps the recipe specifies Cheddar cheese. The strength of Cheddar varies from the insipid and bland to biting and strong. Thus in making the dish, use less or more cheese than called for according to personal preference.

The same could be said for the various kinds of chocolate. Use the chocolate according to taste. Chocolate ranges from mild and sweet to bitter and strong. If on the other hand the recipe spells out the kind of chocolate, such as bittersweet or semisweet, then by all means use the one recommended.

There are some ingredients in recipes that are "critical," however, and should always be measured. These include baking powder and baking soda, things that make pastry or other baked goods heavy or light.

On Peeling Vegetables and Fruits

There are many vegetables and fruits that require peeling or not depending on their use. They include cucumbers, zucchini, carrots, potatoes, apples, and pears, to name the obvious. To peel them, rinse first in cold water and dry with a clean cloth or paper toweling. Then lay out a length of waxed paper, or newspaper if you want to be economical, to catch the peelings. Use a swivel-bladed peeler, going from top to bottom of the vege- table while turning it. The stem and root ends of vegetables may be trimmed away with a small paring knife.

Potatoes when they are peeled are apt to change color as soon as exposed to the air. Thus, if the potatoes are to be peeled in advance of cooking, it is best to let them stand in cold water until ready to use. Apples and pears, too, change color quickly when exposed to the air and should be peeled at the last minute. If they must be peeled in advance, toss them lightly with lemon juice to prevent discoloration.

Tomatoes and peaches are handled similarly; the preferred method of peeling is to drop them into boiling water for exactly twelve seconds. Drain them immediately—but with care so as not to bruise them—in the sink or in a colander. You will now find that with the aid of a small paring knife the skin pulls away easily.

How to Peel an Onion

To peel an onion, cut off a thin slice from the bottom and top. Use a small stainless-steel paring knife (iron discolors the onion flesh) to pull away the outer coating of the onion.

How to Chop an Onion

Place the onion on a chopping board and slice it in half lengthwise with a stainless-steel
kitchen knife.

Place half the onion cut-side
down and slice from right to left
at intervals from ⅛ inch to ½ inch or more depending on
whether you want the onion finely or coarsely chopped. Slice
almost but not quite to the root end.
Give the onion half a quarter turn. Hold
the knife horizontal to the board and
slice once more at intervals from ⅛ inch
to ½ inch or more, slicing from bot-

tom to top. Now, slice downward with the knife at desired intervals, as shown.

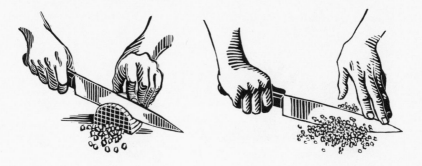

A similar technique could be applied, of course, to any vegetable that needs dicing.

How to Chop Celery

NOTE:
This is a rib.

This is a stalk.

Rinse the stalk and dry it. Trim off the leaves unless the recipe calls for them. Trim off the root end.

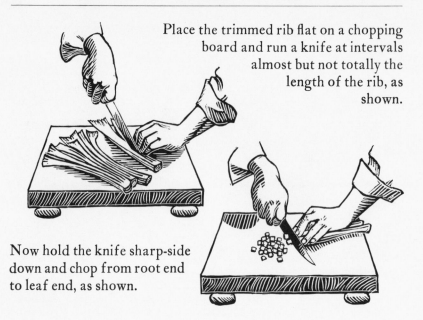

Place the trimmed rib flat on a chopping board and run a knife at intervals almost but not totally the length of the rib, as shown.

Now hold the knife sharp-side down and chop from root end to leaf end, as shown.

How to Chop Parsley

Pull off the green leaves from the tough stems of parsley. Rinse the parsley under cold running water or, if the parsley seems particularly sandy, drop it into cold water and agitate it with the hands. Rinse well and drain. Dry the parsley on toweling, squeezing or pressing lightly.

Place the parsley leaves on a chopping board and gather them closely into the fingers. Push the parsley out from the fingers, chopping with an up-and-down motion of the

chopping knife. After the parsley is thus chopped, continue chopping to the desired degree of fineness.

How to Chop a Carrot

Pare the carrot with a swivel-bladed paring knife. Place the carrot on a flat wooden surface and cut off a very thin slice from one side, as shown. Turn the carrot on this side and cut off another thin slice, as shown.

Continue until the carrot is more or less rectangular like this:

Now split the carrot lengthwise in half. Split each half lengthwise. Gather the four pieces together and chop from right to left, as shown below.

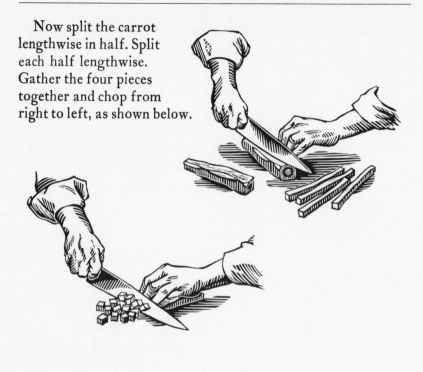

On Raw Onions as an Ingredient

In almost every instance when onions are called for in a recipe, it is best to cook them in butter or oil before adding them to other ingredients. This cooking, until they just lose their inner moisture, without browning does away with the "oniony" taste and they are much more digestible.

On Garlic

This is a
head of garlic . . .

And this is
the spice, clove

made up of
separate cloves

(not to be confused)

How to Chop Garlic with Salt

Place a peeled clove of garlic (or more, if necessary) on a
flat surface and flatten garlic with the flat side of a heavy knife.
To flatten the garlic, simply press down
on the knife with the

heel of one hand. Sprinkle
the garlic with salt and start chopping,
first this way, then that way. Continue chopping
until the garlic is almost a paste.

There are many people, of course, who rely on a garlic press,
but it is this author's considered opinion that the press actually

alters for the worse the flavor of garlic. Garlic put through a press acquires a "metallic" taste.

How to Make Bread Crumbs

Bread crumbs are always best made with bread that is not oven-fresh, i.e., bread that is still fresh yet a few days old. The quickest way to make bread crumbs is in an electric blender. It is not necessary to trim the bread. Cut it into ½-inch cubes and blend small quantities, a cup or so at a time, on high speed.

 As each batch of crumbs is made, empty the blender and continue to make the desired amount. Two slices of bread will yield about ¾ cup of bread crumbs.

On Freshly Grated Cheese

Hard grating cheeses such as Parmesan always taste better if they are freshly grated just before using. In metropolitan areas, at least, wedges of Parmesan cheese are available wherever fine cheeses are sold and at all good Italian groceries. The cheese may be grated, a few cubes at a time, in an electric blender, in a small rotary cheese mill, or on standard upright graters.

On Freshly Ground Pepper

Happily, pepper mills for grinding pepper are becoming increasingly popular in America. Freshly ground pepper tastes far more pungent than that sold commercially ground. There are two kinds of peppercorns used for grating, the black and the white. Black peppercorns are the most popular, but professional chefs generally prefer the white, particularly for white sauces. One reason is that the ground white pepper is not as apparent when added to a white sauce. White pepper is also less pungent and biting than the black.

Blenders are handy, too, for making large quantities of freshly ground pepper.

How to Make Toast

The toast made in an automatic pop-up toaster is acceptable enough for informal meals such as breakfast, but there are better methods of making toast for special occasions.

One method is to preheat the oven to 400 degrees. Trim away and discard the crust from several slices of bread. Brush the trimmed bread generously with melted butter and arrange the bread, buttered-side up, on a baking sheet. Place in the oven and watch carefully. When the bread is golden, turn the slices and continue baking and watching until properly done.

Another method is to brush the bread with butter as indicated, arrange the bread, buttered-side up, on a baking sheet, then place under the broiler. When brown on one side, turn and brown on the other.

NOTE: If desired, line the baking sheet with aluminum foil before adding the bread. This will save washing the baking sheet later.

A Brief Discourse on Spices and Herbs

Spices and herbs are the things that give the greatest nuances in flavor to foods, and without spices and herbs it would be a dull kitchen indeed. A kitchen spice, generally speaking, is a dried seed, bark, or root. The best-known spices include pepper-corns, coriander seeds, ginger root, and the bark of the cinna-mon tree.

Herbs include thyme, bay leaf, parsley, tarragon, and dill. All herbs are best when they are fresh, but dried herbs will, and in the vast majority of cases must, do. Two of the most essential herbs are thyme and bay leaf, the "foundation" herbs of French cookery.

Dried spices and dried herbs age. Consequently, most of them should not be kept on the spice shelf for more than a year or so. Generally speaking, the only way to tell the age of a spice is by its color. A spice like paprika or cayenne pepper is bright red when it is freshest. Later it takes on a dull and brownish look. Green herbs are generally a brilliant green when freshly dried and then they too take on a dullish cast.

Both herbs and spices should be kept in tightly sealed glass jars. They should also be kept away from direct sunlight and heat. Do not keep them over the stove.

On Washing and Draining Foods

It is probably not essential to wash most fruits and vegetables, but it is a good habit to get into. Some vegetables don't require washing, including onions and garlic, of course. Always use cold, clear running water.

The method of washing will depend on the fruit or vegetable. If there is a large quantity to be washed, place them all in the stoppered kitchen sink and add enough water to cover. Rinse and drain. Let common sense dictate whether to drain in a col-ander, sieve, or salad basket. Mushrooms and strawberries, for example, should be drained in a colander or sieve; salad greens in a salad basket. If feasible, salad greens should be shaken in the basket to extract as much of the moisture as possible.

On Draining Foods

A cardboard stiffener, the ordinary kind used by most laundries to protect men's shirts, is extremely useful in the kitchen. Place a stiffener on a flat surface near the stove when cooking bacon, for example. Cover the cardboard with a sheet of absorbent paper toweling, then add the food to be drained.

About Eggs

IT IS TRUE that the flavor of fresh eggs is far superior to those that have been held for an uncommonly long period. But expert tasters in the food field can rarely distinguish the difference in the taste of newly laid eggs and those that have been kept refrigerated for two weeks.

Refrigeration is the key word. Eggs that have been refrigerated for three weeks taste better than eggs held for three days at room temperature.

In most recipes it is preferable to take eggs from the refrigerator and let them come to room temperature before using. But eggs to be fried in a skillet will spread less if they are cold, which is desirable.

If two eggs of a different age are broken onto two different plates, it is easy to tell which is the fresher. The yolk of the fresher egg will stand higher and be more rounded; the whites of both will, of course, be liquid, but the white of the fresher egg will be more "firm."

There is, oddly enough, one instance in egg cookery when the freshest eggs are not necessarily the most desirable: eggs that are a week or so old will peel better after they are hard-cooked.

Except in the case of an omelette, which must be produced in seconds, eggs respond best to slow cooking, whether you are poaching eggs or making a custard.

The best materials to use for cooking eggs are aluminum, stainless steel, or enamel-coated cast iron. Those new nonstick

skillets that permit cooking without fats are all right for anyone who for one reason or another is on a diet. But nothing
glorifies the flavor of eggs like butter.

How to Crack an Egg

To crack an egg, gently but firmly tap the middle of the egg
against a hard surface such as the edge
of a table, the rim of a heavy bowl,
or the kitchen sink.

Hold the egg over a mixing
bowl and break the egg in half,
using the fingers of both hands.

If the egg is to be
separated, use half the eggshell as the cup
which retains the yolk. Gently shift the yolk from one half of
the shell to the other, letting the white fall into the mixing bowl.

Finally, run the forefinger around the rim of the shell
to completely catch the egg white and drop
the egg yolk into a mixing bowl, saucepan,
or whatever utensil it is to be used in.

IMPORTANT THINGS TO KNOW ABOUT EGG WHITES, YOLKS, AND SHELLS

Egg whites will not become foamy or stiff if there is one single trace of egg yolk mixed in with them. Therefore, break your eggs with care.

If, by accident, a small bit of yolk falls into the whites, try to scoop it out with HALF A BROKEN EGGSHELL. If the yolk is smeared on the side of a mixing bowl, wipe it off with a clean cloth.

If, by chance, a small bit of eggshell falls into a batch of egg whites or yolks or a mixture of both, it is easy to remove it, again, with HALF A BROKEN EGGSHELL.

About Egg Yolks

Egg yolks, like flour and cornstarch, are a thickening agent for sauces, custards, and the like. For fact collectors, it might be noted that 2 egg yolks are approximately equal to 1 tablespoon of flour as a thickener.

Unlike flour and cornstarch, egg yolks must be treated with special care, for an obvious reason. High heat affects both yolks and whites in the most visible manner when scrambled together in a skillet. In exactly the same way high heat affects egg yolks in a sauce. If the yolk blended in the sauce is brought to an excessive temperature, the yolk "scrambles," just as it does in the skillet, and causes the sauce to curdle. Therefore, when yolks are used to thicken sauces they must be cooked over very gentle heat.

On Heating Yolks

Some people think the best way to control this heat is by using a double boiler with the sauce in the top and simmering water in the bottom. A more expeditious way to control the heat, however, is to place an asbestos pad or metal disk known as a Flame Tamer over the heat. Then place the saucepan on the pad or disk and continue making the sauce over low heat. The pad or disk distributes the heat more evenly over the bottom of the pan and decreases the danger of curdling. Take care, however, to stir the sauce constantly, using a wooden spoon and moving it this way and that way all over the bottom of the saucepan. All areas of the bottom should be covered to prevent the sauce from sticking.

On Adding Yolks to Thicken a Sauce

When yolks are to be added to a sauce to thicken it at the last moment, they are generally blended lightly with cream before adding. The way to proceed is this: beat the yolks and stir in the cream. When blended, add a little of the hot sauce to the cream and egg-yolk mixture to raise the temperature of the latter. Now, add this mixture to the sauce while stirring with a whisk over low heat. Stir constantly until the sauce is thickened but do not boil.

On Beating Egg Whites

When egg whites are to be beaten for a cake, soufflé, or whatever, they will achieve more volume if they are at room temperature. They may be beaten with a wire whisk, a hand rotary beater, or an electric mixer.

Professional chefs maintain that the most effective method of beating whites is by hand, using a copper bowl and a wire whisk. Although this is true, it is not practical for most home cooks because it requires a strong right arm and endurance. For all practical purposes, an electric mixer is thoroughly suitable.

Make note that egg whites should be beaten at the last minute before they are used, otherwise they become deflated and moist.

How to Tell a Hard-Cooked Egg from a Raw Egg

If, by chance, you have both hard-cooked eggs and raw eggs in the shell in the refrigerator, there is a simple method for telling which is which. Gently set an egg down on a large flat surface and carefully spin it around. If it spins around neatly more or less in one spot, it is a raw egg. If it spins around in a wayward, haphazard style, it is a hard-cooked egg.

HOW TO SCRAMBLE EGGS

For 4 servings, break 8 eggs into a mixing bowl and beat vigorously with an ordinary dinner fork or a wire whisk until thoroughly blended. Add 1 tablespoon of heavy cream and salt and pepper to taste. Melt 3 or 4 tablespoons of butter in a 9-inch skillet (not a black iron skillet), and when the butter is frothy but not brown add the eggs. Cook gently, pushing with a rubber spatula from the outside edge of the eggs toward the center of the skillet. The eggs should be served instantly while they are still soft and creamy. Remember also that unless the eggs are served immediately they will continue to cook from the retained heat of the skillet.

SCRAMBLED EGGS WITH TARRAGON

Before adding beaten eggs to the skillet as in the preceding recipe, add approximately ½ to 1 teaspoon of chopped tarragon for each 2 eggs. Remember that dried tarragon is considerably stronger than fresh and that the pungency of even fresh herbs varies. That is why approximate herb measurements are given.

SCRAMBLED EGGS WITH ANCHOVY

4 slices buttered fresh toast   8 to 12 eggs
4 teaspoons anchovy paste   Parsley sprigs for garnish

First spread each slice of toast lightly with anchovy paste before making the eggs. As soon as the eggs are scrambled spoon onto the toast and garnish the center of each serving with a parsley sprig.

Yield: Four servings.

HOW TO "BOIL" EGGS

The word "boil" is misused as applied to cooking eggs. The eggs should not boil; they should simmer. The cooking time for the eggs depends on various factors, such as how large the eggs are and how cold they are. Preferably they should be at room temperature.

To soft-cook eggs:
Place the eggs in a saucepan and add cold water to cover. Bring the water to a boil and reduce the heat to simmer. For medium-sized eggs, cook them for 5 to 6 minutes from the time the water comes to a boil.

To hard-cook eggs:
Simmer them for 12 to 15 minutes. When the eggs are

cooked, plunge them immediately into cold water to facilitate peeling. If the eggs are difficult to peel it is probably because they are too fresh.

Eggs that are particularly large or chilled from recent refrigeration should be cooked a minute or two longer than indicated here.

STUFFED EGGS

6 hard-cooked eggs
3 anchovy fillets, finely chopped, or 1 tablespoon anchovy paste
1 tablespoon finely chopped chives
3 tablespoons butter, at room temperature
1 teaspoon lemon juice
1 teaspoon olive oil
½ teaspoon Worcestershire sauce
⅛ teaspoon cayenne pepper
1 tablespoon or more mayonnaise

1. Crack the eggshells thoroughly and hold eggs under cold running water while peeling. Dry them on paper toweling. Place the eggs on a flat surface and cut them in half either lengthwise or crosswise. Gently empty the yolks into a sieve or small strainer and, using the fingers, press the yolks through the sieve into a mixing bowl. Add the remaining ingredients, using just enough mayonnaise to bind. Blend thoroughly with a fork.

2. Spoon the mixture into the cavities of the whites, or use a pastry tube. For the latter, fit a pastry bag with a "star" tube. Fill the bottom of the bag with the yolk mixture, then twist the top of the bag. Hold the tube inside the cavity and press the bag to extract as much filling as desired. When the cavity is filled, quickly lift the bag and a star pattern should remain. The eggs are ready to be served now or they may be decorated.

3. To decorate the stuffed eggs, place one caper on the

top of each stuffed egg. Or decorate with cutouts of pimiento, olives, green pepper, or truffles. Cutouts are made with what are known as fancy cutters or truffle cutters, available wherever fine cookware is sold and in many department stores. The cutters shape small stars, crescents, squares, rounds, and the like.

Yield: 12 stuffed eggs.

HOW TO BAKE EGGS

This is a customary way of serving eggs in European households. It is excellent for a leisurely breakfast or brunch.

6 teaspoons butter	Salt and freshly ground
¾ cup heavy cream	black pepper to taste
6 to 12 eggs	Parsley sprigs
	Buttered toast

1. Preheat the oven to 375 degrees.

2. Arrange six ovenproof ramekins (small, low, round baking dishes) in a baking pan and pour boiling water around them. The water should be about ½ inch deep in the pan. Keep the water simmering over low heat on top of the stove.

3. Add 1 teaspoon of butter to each ramekin and when melted add 1 tablespoon of cream. Break 1 or 2 eggs into each ramekin and top each with another tablespoon of cream.

4. Sprinkle with salt and pepper and bake for 8 to 12 minutes. The time will depend on the size of the eggs. When the eggs are done the yolks will still be liquid and the whites barely set. Do not forget that the eggs will continue to cook slightly when removed from the oven due to the retained heat in the ramekins. Garnish with parsley sprigs and serve with buttered toast.

Yield: Six servings.

BAKED EGGS WITH MUSHROOMS

12 medium-sized mushrooms	Salt and freshly ground black pepper to taste
2 tablespoons butter	1/4 cup heavy cream
Lemon juice	

1. Wash the mushrooms under cold running water, then dry them on a clean cloth.

2. Chop the mushrooms finely. Melt the butter in a saucepan and add the mushrooms. Sprinkle lightly with a

few drops of lemon juice and cook, stirring, until all the moisture disappears. Add the seasonings and cream.

3. Following the preceding recipe for baked eggs, place one sixth of the mushroom mixture on top of 1 teaspoon of butter and 1 tablespoon of cream in each ramekin, then top with the eggs and remaining cream. Bake and serve as indicated.

Yield: Six servings.

HOW TO POACH AN EGG

Fill an aluminum, stainless-steel, or enamel-coated skillet almost to the brim with water. Add 1 teaspoon or so of white vinegar to the water and bring to a boil. Now add the eggs one at a time. The most sure-fire way of doing this is to break each egg into a small saucer, then gently slide the egg off the saucer and into the boiling water. With a little practice, however, it is more efficient to break the egg directly into the water. To do this, crack the egg-shell gently, then, using the fingers of both hands, break the shell, holding the egg quite close to the simmering water.

Simmer the eggs gently until the white is solidly white and no longer transparent; the yolk must remain runny. It takes approximately 2½ to 3 minutes to poach an egg.

The time depends on the size of the eggs and the temperature of the eggs when added to the water.

When the eggs are cooked, use a slotted spoon or a slotted pancake turner to remove them. Drain on absorbent paper toweling.

1. The vinegar helps "set" the whites as they cook.

2. Do not use a black iron skillet to poach eggs because it may impart a metallic taste and rusty look to the eggs.

3. The eggs are best served immediately. In unusual circumstances, however, the eggs may be reheated briefly in simmering salted water after they are cooked.

HOW TO MAKE AN OMELETTE

The most important thing about omelette-making is the pan. It should be a heavy pan with curved sides, an unmarred surface and, for most home purposes, a nonmetallic handle. Sizes of omelette pans vary from one for a two-egg omelette to those for forty eggs. The ideal size for home use is a pan for a two-egg omelette or a three-egg omelette. A pan with a 6-inch bottom is suitable for two eggs; a 7- or 8-inch bottom for three.

When the pan is first purchased it must be treated. First scrub well with a non-metallic scouring pad and rinse well. Dry and add approximately ½ inch of oil to the pan and set it over moderate heat. Let stand just to the point where the oil starts to smoke. Let the oil cool in the pan and then discard the oil. Wipe the inside of the pan well with paper toweling and it is ready for use.

After each session of omelette-making the pan should be wiped with paper toweling and a little table salt. If the pan has not been used in some time, it is best to wash it, wipe with paper toweling and a little salt, then brush with oil.

1. For each omelette, break 2 or 3 fresh eggs into a

mixing bowl. Add a bit
of salt and beat well
with a table fork.

2. Meanwhile, place the
omelette pan over moderate
to high heat. The pan should be
heated so that the butter, when
added, will melt immediately
but without burning. The classic
test for temperature is to flick, with
the fingers, a few drops of water into the pan;
if the drops skitter around quickly, the pan is hot enough.
When the pan is hot enough, add 1 tablespoon of butter,
using a fresh table fork. Swirl the butter around in the pan
to cover the bottom and sides and quickly add the eggs.

3. Grasp the pan handle with the left hand and shake in
a fore-and-aft motion. Simultaneously, stir the eggs around
in the pan, with the fork held more or less parallel to the
bottom of the pan. Use a circular motion and try not to
scrape the bottom. Remember that the omelette
must be made in seconds, no more than
30 seconds at the outside.

4. When the omelette is still
very moist in the center but
firm on the bottom, raise the
handle to tilt the pan. Give a

quick, forceful knock near the point where the handle
joins the pan and this will force the omelette toward the
bottom of the pan. If there is a filling, it should be hot and
ready. Add it to the center of the omelette, which should,
at this point, be curved slightly. With a
table fork push and fold the edges of
the omelette toward the center.

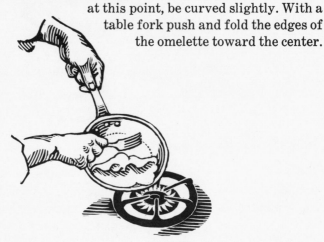

5. Drop the table fork
and transfer the handle of the pan to the right hand.
Quickly cover the pan with a hot plate, then,
presto, set the plate upright
while simultaneously
inverting the omelette
pan over its center.

6. The omelette should fall into the center of the plate. Ideally the omelette's ends should be pointed. This effect can be encouraged with a fork or with the fingers.

Yield: 1 omelette.

MUSHROOM OMELETTE

For each omelette, slice 2 or 3 mushrooms and cook, stirring, in 1 tablespoon of butter. Sprinkle with salt, pepper, and chopped parsley and use as an omelette filling.

OMELETTE AUX FINES HERBES

One of the best-known omelettes is called *aux fines herbes*. The classic *fines herbes* are parsley, tarragon, chives, and chervil. They are chopped in equal quantities and either stirred into the eggs before the omelette is made or sprinkled in the center of the omelette before it is folded. Use about 1 tablespoon of the combined herbs (chervil is comparatively rare in this country so use any combination of the four herbs available) for each omelette.

CHEESE OMELETTE

Use 1/4 to 1/2 cup of grated cheese, such as Cheddar, Swiss, or Gruyère, as a filling for omelettes, sprinkling it in the center of the omelette before it is folded.

HOW TO FRY AN EGG

Almost any kind of fat may be used for frying eggs but the commonest are butter, salad oil—such as peanut or vegetable oil—or bacon fat. Butter and bacon fat produce a flavor that many people prefer, but salad oil will give the whitest, best-looking egg.

Whatever fat is used, the procedure is the same.

1. For each 6 eggs, heat 3 tablespoons of fat. When the fat is hot but not burning, carefully break the eggs into the skillet. Gently spoon the fat over the eggs as they cook.

2. Cook the eggs over gentle heat until the whites are set and the yolks are still liquid. If the eggs are to be cooked on both sides, turn them carefully with a pancake turner and serve immediately.

Yield: Three to six servings.

FRIED EGGS WITH BLACK BUTTER

Follow the preceding recipe for fried eggs but add 4 tablespoons of butter to a separate skillet. Cook over moderate heat until the butter is dark brown. Add approximately 1 tablespoon of vinegar and pour over the eggs. Sprinkle with parsley and capers and serve hot.

THE TRUTH ABOUT SOUFFLÉS

The method for making almost all main-course soufflés is approximately the same, and anyone who learns the technique can vary the soufflé at will. The basis for these soufflés is a simple white sauce to which a solid of some sort is added. The solid may be a seafood (such as flaked crab or chopped shrimp) or a cheese or, as in one of the recipes that follows, mushrooms. To this egg yolks are added. They are cooked briefly without boiling. These eggs yolks, as always, tend to thicken a sauce. Remember, too much heat may curdle the yolks.

The thing that makes a soufflé puff are the beaten egg whites that are folded in. When these whites are exposed to the oven heat, the globules expand and give the soufflé its gossamer texture. The easiest most sure-fire way to add the whites is this: stir in half the whites until they are well incorporated in the sauce, then gently fold in the remaining whites with a rubber spatula. Make sure the spatula cuts down into the mixture, scrapes down to the bottom then up again. The whites must not be folded in too thoroughly. If a few specks of white still show, that is all right too.

To make a soufflé, use a straight-sided soufflé dish. The interior of the dish—bottom and sides—should be buttered so the soufflé can slip up the sides as it bakes.

There are no great mysteries involved in the making of soufflés. Actually, they are quite easy to make if a few simple directions are followed. There are many ways to make soufflés and almost no two cookbooks will duplicate the process. I have personally found the following things to result in a perfect soufflé.

1. There is much discussion as to whether soufflé dishes should

be buttered before using. They should be and they should also be chilled in the refrigerator or briefly in the freezer before the soufflé mixture is added.

2. The basic mixture for a soufflé is a simple white sauce. However, less butter should be used than normally in making the sauce. For a perfect soufflé, the sauce should be unusually thick. This is achieved by making the sauce with lots of flour in relation to the amount of milk. A little more thickening with cornstarch helps. The sauce is further thickened with egg yolks. And here is a point that few recipes make. The sauce, after the yolks are added, must be cooked ever so briefly. After the

yolks are added, the sauce is brought to a boil only for seconds, and at this point the sauce must be stirred rapidly, preferably with a wire whisk.

3. The egg whites must be beaten until stiff and stand in peaks. Half the whites are whisked into the sauce. The remainder are carefully folded in with a rubber spatula. The mixture is now ready to pour into the prepared dish.

4. The soufflé must be cooked in a preheated oven. The oven temperature may range from about 350 degrees to 400 degrees and the temperature will, naturally, affect the cooking time. The higher the temperature, the more rapidly the soufflé will cook.

5. A classic soufflé is light, delicate, and quite moist in the center when it is done. Some people, however, prefer a firmer center (and therefore cook the soufflé longer).

6. As to the size of the soufflé dish, it may be large or small. The important thing is to have it completely filled with the soufflé mixture before baking. The best soufflé dishes are white ceramic rather than metal.

CURRIED SEAFOOD SOUFFLÉ

5 tablespoons butter
1 cup fresh, frozen, or
   canned crab meat or
   other seafood
3 tablespoons finely
   chopped onion
½ teaspoon minced
   garlic
3 tablespoons finely
   chopped celery
6 tablespoons flour

1 tablespoon curry powder
2 cups milk
Salt and freshly ground
   black pepper to taste
1 tablespoon cornstarch
1 tablespoon water
⅛ teaspoon cayenne
   pepper
¼ teaspoon Worcester-
   shire sauce
8 eggs

1. Preheat the oven to 400 degrees.

2. Using the fingers, rub the inside of a 2-quart soufflé dish with 1 tablespoon of the butter. Make certain the butter covers all the bottom and sides. Place the dish briefly in the freezer or refrigerate until ready to use.

3. Place the crab in a mixing bowl and carefully pick over the crab to remove all traces of shell or cartilage. Set crab aside.

4. Melt the remaining butter in a saucepan. Add the onion, garlic, and celery and cook over moderate heat, stirring constantly, until the onion is wilted; do not let it brown. Add the flour and curry powder and keep on stirring around and around until the flour is blended with the other ingredients.

5. Add the milk, stirring constantly and rapidly with a wire whisk. Continue cooking and stirring until the sauce is thickened and smooth. Season to taste with salt and pepper. Continue cooking and stirring over low heat for about 1 minute. The sauce should be quite thick.

6. In a small bowl blend together the cornstarch and water and add to the sauce, stirring constantly. Continue cooking for about 1 minute. Add the cayenne pepper and Worcestershire sauce.

7. Break the eggs, one at a time, letting the whites fall into a mixing bowl. Drop the yolks into another small mixing bowl.

8. Using a rubber spatula, add the yolks to the sauce and beat rapidly with the whisk. Return the sauce to the heat and cook over low heat, stirring. Let the sauce bubble, stirring constantly, for about 3 seconds, no longer.

9. Using a rubber spatula, transfer the sauce to a round-bottomed mixing bowl. Stir in the picked-over crab meat and let the sauce cool for about 10 minutes at room temperature.

10. Beat the egg whites with a wire whisk, rotary beater, or electric mixer until they are quite stiff and stand in peaks. (It is all right to add the beaten egg whites to the sauce while the sauce is warm BUT NOT HOT.) Scoop half the beaten egg whites into the sauce and whisk them well into the sauce, using a rubber spatula or a wire whisk.

11. Scoop the remaining whites into the sauce. Using a cutting-in motion with a rubber spatula, cut down to the bottom, scoop around the bottom and bring the spatula up. Do this several times. Do not overfold or the soufflé will not puff properly. Leave some white specks showing.

12. Using the spatula, pour the mixture into the prepared soufflé dish. Place the soufflé in the oven and immediately turn the oven heat to 375 degrees. Bake for 30 to 40 minutes. Some people like a soufflé with a moist interior and for this the soufflé should be baked for the shorter period of time. For a soufflé with a firmer interior, use the longer cooking time.

Yield: Six to eight servings.

NOTE: You may substitute almost any cooked seafood for the crab meat. This would include lobster, shrimp, salmon, or leftover fish. The seafood should be cut into small, bite-size pieces before it is added to the sauce.

TARRAGON CHEESE SOUFFLÉ

3 tablespoons butter
⅓ cup plus 1 tablespoon
   grated Parmesan
   cheese
3 tablespoons flour
1 cup milk
2 teaspoons cornstarch
1 tablespoon water
⅔ cup grated Swiss,

Gruyère, or Cheddar
   cheese
Salt and freshly ground
   black pepper to taste
⅛ teaspoon cayenne
   pepper
1 teaspoon chopped fresh
   tarragon or ½ tea-
   spoon dried tarragon
6 eggs

1. Preheat the oven to 400 degrees.

2. Using the fingers, rub the inside of a 1½- quart soufflé dish with 1 tablespoon of the butter. Make certain the butter covers all the bottom and sides. Sprinkle 1 tablespoon of the grated Parmesan cheese into the dish. Shake the cheese around inside the dish until the bottom and sides are lightly coated. Place the dish briefly in the freezer or refrigerate until ready to use.

3. Melt the remaining butter in a saucepan. Stir in the flour, using a wire whisk. When the mixture is blended, add the milk, stirring rapidly with the whisk. Bring the sauce to a boil, stirring constantly. When the mixture is thickened and smooth, continue cooking and stirring for about 1 minute.

4. In a small bowl, blend together the cornstarch and water and add to the sauce, stirring constantly. Continue

cooking for about 1 minute. Remove the sauce from the heat and stir in the grated Swiss, Gruyère, or Cheddar cheese. Add the remaining Parmesan cheese. Stir until the cheeses are blended into the sauce. Season to taste with salt and pepper. Stir in the cayenne pepper and tarragon.

5. Break the eggs, one at a time, letting the whites fall into a mixing bowl. Drop the yolks into another small mixing bowl.

6. Using a rubber spatula, add the yolks to the sauce and beat rapidly with the whisk. Return the sauce to the heat and cook over very low heat, stirring. Let the sauce bubble, stirring constantly, for about 3 seconds, no longer.

7. Using a rubber spatula, transfer the sauce to a round-bottomed mixing bowl. Let the sauce cool for about 10 minutes at room temperature.

8. Beat the egg whites with a wire whisk, rotary beater, or electric mixer until they are quite stiff and stand in peaks. (It is all right to add the beaten egg whites to the sauce while the sauce is warm BUT NOT HOT.) Scoop half the beaten egg whites into the sauce and whisk them well into the sauce, using a rubber spatula or a wire whisk.

9. Scoop the remaining whites into the sauce. Using a cutting-in motion with a rubber spatula, cut down to the bottom, scoop around the bottom and bring the spatula up. Do this several times. Do not overfold or the soufflé will not puff properly. Leave some white specks showing.

10. Using the spatula, pour the mixture into the prepared soufflé dish. Place the soufflé in the oven and immediately turn the oven heat to 375 degrees. Bake 25 to 35 minutes. Some people like a soufflé with a moist interior and for this the soufflé should be baked for the shorter period of time. For a soufflé with a firmer interior, use the longer cooking time.

Yield: Four to six servings.

MUSHROOM SOUFFLÉ

5 tablespoons butter
½ pound fresh mush-
    rooms
Salt and freshly ground
    black pepper to taste
¼ teaspoon nutmeg

3 tablespoons flour
1 cup milk
2 teaspoons cornstarch
1 tablespoon water
6 eggs

1. Preheat the oven to 400 degrees.

2. Using the fingers, rub the inside of a 1½-quart soufflé dish with 1 tablespoon of the butter. Make certain the butter covers all the bottom and sides. Place the dish briefly in the freezer or refrigerate until ready to use.

3. Using a large knife and on a flat surface, slice the mushrooms. Cut the slices into thin strips. Chop the strips into tiny cubes.

4. Heat 2 tablespoons of the remaining butter in a saucepan or skillet and add the chopped mushrooms. Cook, stirring with a wooden spoon, until the mushrooms give up their juices. This should take about 3 minutes. Season the mushrooms with salt, pepper, and nutmeg and set aside.

5. Melt the remaining butter in a saucepan. Stir in the flour, using a wire whisk. When the mixture is blended, add the milk, stirring rapidly with the whisk. Bring the sauce to a boil, stirring constantly. When the mixture is thickened and smooth, continue cooking and stirring for about 1 minute.

6. In a small bowl, blend together the cornstarch and water and add to the sauce, stirring constantly. Continue cooking for about 1 minute. Stir in the chopped mushrooms. Season to taste with salt and pepper.

7. Break the eggs, one at a time, letting the whites fall

into a mixing bowl. Drop the yolks into another small mixing bowl.

8. Using a rubber spatula, scrape the yolks into the sauce and beat rapidly with the whisk. Return the sauce to the heat and cook over low heat, stirring. Let the sauce bubble, stirring constantly, for about 3 seconds, no longer.

9. Using a rubber spatula, transfer the sauce to a round-bottomed mixing bowl. Let the sauce cool for about 10 minutes at room temperature.

10. Beat the egg whites with a wire whisk, rotary beater, or electric mixer until they are quite stiff and stand in peaks. (It is all right to add the beaten egg whites to the sauce while the sauce is warm BUT NOT HOT.) Scoop half the beaten egg whites into the sauce and whisk them well into the sauce, using a rubber spatula or a wire whisk.

11. Scoop the remaining whites into the sauce. Using a cutting-in motion with a rubber spatula, cut down to the bottom, scoop around the bottom and bring the spatula up. Do this several times. Do not overfold or the soufflé will not puff properly. Leave some white specks showing.

12. Using the spatula, pour the mixture into the prepared soufflé dish. Place the soufflé in the oven and immediately turn the oven heat to 375 degrees. Bake for 25 to 35 minutes. Some people like a soufflé with a moist interior and for this the soufflé should be baked for the shorter period of time. For a soufflé with a firmer interior, use the longer cooking time.

Yield: Four to six servings.

SALMON SOUFFLÉ

3 tablespoons butter
3 tablespoons flour
1 cup milk
2 teaspoons cornstarch
1 tablespoon water
Salt to taste
Cayenne pepper to taste

¼ teaspoon nutmeg
6 eggs
1 cup freshly cooked salmon or a 7-ounce can of salmon, drained, with skin and bones removed

1. Preheat the oven to 400 degrees.

2. Using the fingers, rub the inside of a 1½-quart soufflé dish with 1 tablespoon of the butter. Make certain the butter covers all the bottom and sides. Place the dish briefly in the freezer or refrigerate until ready to use.

3. Melt the remaining butter in a saucepan. Stir in the flour, using a wire whisk. When the mixture is blended, add the milk, stirring rapidly with the whisk. Bring the sauce to a boil, stirring constantly. When the mixture is thickened and smooth, continue cooking and stirring for about 1 minute.

4. In a small bowl, blend together the cornstarch and water and add to the sauce, stirring constantly. Continue cooking for about 1 minute. Season to taste with salt and cayenne pepper. Add the nutmeg.

5. Break the eggs, one at a time, letting the whites fall into a mixing bowl. Drop the yolks into another small mixing bowl.

6. Using a rubber spatula, add the yolks to the sauce and beat rapidly with the whisk. Return the sauce to the heat and cook over very low heat, stirring. Let the sauce bubble, stirring constantly, for about 3 seconds, no longer. Flake the salmon with the fingers and stir into the sauce.

7. Using a rubber spatula, transfer the sauce to a round-bottomed mixing bowl. Let the sauce cool for about 10 minutes at room temperature.

8. Beat the egg whites with a wire whisk, rotary beater, or electric mixer until they are quite stiff and stand in peaks. (It is all right to add the beaten egg whites to the sauce while the sauce is warm BUT NOT HOT.) Scoop half the beaten egg whites into the sauce and whisk them well into the sauce, using a rubber spatula or a wire whisk.

9. Scoop the remaining whites into the sauce. Using a cutting-in motion with a rubber spatula, cut down to the bottom, scoop around the bottom and bring the spatula up. Do this several times. Do not overfold or the soufflé will not puff properly. Leave some white specks showing.

10. Using the spatula, pour the mixture into the prepared soufflé dish. Place the soufflé in the oven and immediately turn the oven down to 375 degrees. Bake for 25 to 35 minutes. Some people like a soufflé with a moist interior and for this the soufflé should be baked for the shorter period of time. For a soufflé with a firmer interior, use the longer cooking time.

Yield: Four to six servings.

SAUCES AND SOUPS

The Virtues of the Versatile Cream Sauce
and Dishes to Sauce . . . The Oil and Butter
Sauces and Their Uses . . . Tomato Sauces and
Variations . . . Examples of the Three Basic Types
of Soups—Clear, Cream, and Vegetable or
Peasant Soups

Sauces

WHITE SAUCE

By far the most important sauce in Western cuisine is what is known variously as white sauce, cream sauce, and *velouté*. There are only five essentials for making the basic sauce: butter, flour, a liquid, a saucepan, and something to stir with. The best thing to stir with is a wire whisk.

If you will study the following you will know all there is to know about making this sauce.

1½ tablespoons butter   1 cup milk
1½ tablespoons flour

1. For this quantity of sauce use a 3- or 4-cup saucepan. Place it on the stove and add the butter. Heat the butter and when it is melted add the flour. Stir with a wire whisk until the flour is blended.

2. Add the milk gradually, stirring this way and that with the whisk. The whisk should move all over the bottom and sides of the saucepan. Once the technique of sauce-making is learned, it is possible to add the milk all at once, but you must stir vigorously to prevent the sauce from lumping. Stir constantly until the sauce boils. When it boils the sauce is made and it has reached its maximum thickness. At this point the sauce can be used but it will taste better if it is cooked over low heat, stirring occasionally, for 5 to 10 minutes longer. Once cooked, the sauce

is ready to be seasoned and combined with other ingredients.

Yield: About 1 cup.

☞ IMPORTANT! READ THIS:

A white sauce is nothing short of miraculous for there is literally no end to its uses and variations. It is the basis for cheese sauces and creamed dishes as well as soufflés.

The thing that thickens a white sauce is flour; the thing that thins it is a liquid, such as milk, cream, or broth. One tablespoon of flour for 1 cup of liquid will give a very thin white sauce. Three tablespoons of flour for 1 cup of liquid will give a very thick white sauce. If a sauce is too thick, it is quite easy to make it thinner by adding more liquid. Add the liquid gradually, stirring, until the sauce is as thin as you want it. But if the sauce is too thin, don't try to add more plain flour; instead, melt a little butter in a separate saucepan and then stir in an equal amount of flour and whisk until blended. Now add the sauce gradually, stirring all the time. Another way to thicken a sauce is to blend equal parts butter with flour, 1 teaspoon of each, let us say. Use the fingers to blend the two. Add this, bit by bit, to the boiling sauce, stirring as it is added. Continue adding this mixture to the desired thickness. Remember that the sauce thickens immediately after the flour is added.

DISHES TO MAKE WITH WHITE SAUCE

If you will look at them closely, you will see a marked resemblance in the group of recipes that follow. All are based on the "medium" white or cream sauce principle; that is, they are made with 1½ tablespoons of flour for each cup of liquid. Therefore they are not as thin as the sauce for boiled beef given on page 79.

This formula—1½ tablespoons of flour for 1 cup of milk or a combination of milk and cream—is just about ideal for almost all creamed dishes. Recipes follow for some of the best-known creamed dishes—creamed ham, creamed tuna or salmon, curried eggs, to name a few. There is also a recipe for eggs *à la tripe,* which is nothing more than creamed eggs with onions.

The basic rule for making any creamed dish is to use 1 cup of cream sauce for each 2 cups of solids. For example, the recipe for creamed ham calls for 1 cup of the cream sauce plus 2 cups of diced ham. Thus, if you want to make creamed shrimp, crab, lobster, or whatever, use 1 cup of sauce with 2 cups of cubed shrimp, crab, lobster, or whatever. The "whatever" might, of course, include vegetables, such as onions, carrots, or Brussels sprouts. And all these vegetables should be well drained before adding to a sauce or the liquid left on them will tend to thin the sauce.

CREAMED HAM

1½ tablespoons butter
1½ tablespoons flour
¾ cup milk
¼ cup heavy cream
Freshly ground pepper
  to taste

¾ pound cooked, sliced
  ham, approximately
Worcestershire sauce
  (optional)
4 slices toast
For garnish: paprika,
  4 parsley sprigs

1. Heat the butter in a 3- or 4-cup saucepan and when the butter is melted add the flour. Stir with a wire whisk and when blended add the milk gradually, stirring with the

whisk. When thickened and smooth stir in the cream and season with pepper. Do not salt this sauce at this point because the ham will provide the salt. Cook the sauce, stirring occasionally, for 3 minutes.

2. Cut the ham into small cubes. There should be about 2 cups loosely packed. Add it to the sauce and stir gently. Heat thoroughly. If the sauce seems too thick, you may thin it by adding heavy cream, a little at a time, until the sauce is as thin as desired.

3. Taste the sauce. If it needs salt, add a little. You may also add a touch of Worcestershire sauce for flavor. When ready to serve, place a slice of toast on each of four warm plates. Spoon the creamed ham onto the toast and sprinkle each serving lightly with paprika. Place a small sprig of parsley in the center of each serving. Serve immediately. Buttered peas and sliced tomatoes seasoned with salt and pepper go very well with this dish.

Yield: Four servings.

Variation: Add ½ cup cooked green peas to the preceding recipe along with the ham.

CREAMED CHICKEN

1½ tablespoons butter
1½ tablespoons flour
¾ cup fresh or canned
  chicken broth
¼ cup heavy cream
Salt and freshly ground
  pepper to taste

2 cups skinless, boneless
  cooked chicken, cubed
4 slices toast
4 parsley sprigs for
  garnish

1. Heat the butter in a 3- or 4-cup saucepan and when butter is melted add the flour. Stir with a wire whisk and when blended add the chicken stock gradually. When thick-

ened and smooth stir in the cream and season with salt and pepper. Be careful in adding salt, however, because the chicken stock may have enough already.

2. Add the chicken pieces and heat thoroughly. If the sauce seems too thick, you may thin it by adding heavy cream, a little at a time, until the sauce is as thin as desired.

3. When ready to serve, place a slice of toast on each of four warm plates. Spoon the creamed chicken onto the toast and place a small sprig of parsley in the center of each serving. Serve immediately. As with the creamed ham, buttered peas and sliced tomatoes seasoned with salt and pepper go very well with this dish.

Yield: Four servings.

CREAMED TUNA OR SALMON

1½ tablespoons butter	Salt and freshly ground
1½ tablespoons flour	pepper to taste
3 tablespoons chopped	2 seven-ounce cans solid-
onion	pack tuna or
¾ cup milk	salmon
¼ cup heavy cream	

1. Heat the butter in a 3- or 4-cup saucepan and add the onion. Cook, stirring with a wire whisk, until the onion is wilted. Do not brown the onion.

2. Sprinkle the onion with the flour and continue cooking and stirring briefly until blended. Add the milk gradually, stirring with the whisk. When blended and smooth add the cream and stir. When thickened and smooth add salt and pepper to taste. Simmer for 3 minutes, stirring occasionally.

3. Drain the cans of tuna or salmon and empty the fish into a mixing bowl. Flake with a fork but leave bite-sized

chunks. Add the chunks to the sauce. Heat thoroughly.
Serve on toast, if desired, or with rice.
Yield: Two to four servings.

Variation: Cook ½ cup finely minced celery and 2 tablespoons finely minced green pepper with 1 tablespoon butter
in a small skillet. Cook just until celery is crisp-tender.
Add this to the above sauce along with the tuna.

EGGS À LA TRIPE

1 small onion
1½ tablespoons butter
1½ tablespoons flour
¾ cup milk
¼ cup heavy cream
Salt and freshly ground
    pepper to taste

⅛ teaspoon cayenne
    pepper
¼ teaspoon nutmeg
4 hard-cooked eggs
    (*see page 39*)

1. Peel the onion and, using a sharp stainless-steel knife,
cut the onion into the thinnest-possible slices to make
almost-transparent onion rings. There should be about ½
cup of onion rings.
2. Heat the butter in a 4-cup saucepan and when butter
is hot add the onion rings. Cover tightly and cook over low
heat until onion is wilted. Sprinkle the onion rings with
the flour and stir to distribute the flour evenly. Gradually
stir in the milk, using a wire whisk. Bring to a boil, stirring, and when thickened and smooth add the cream and
stir. Add salt and pepper to taste. Add the cayenne and
nutmeg. Simmer for about 3 minutes.
3. Meanwhile, peel the eggs under cold running water
and dry on paper toweling. Slice the eggs with an egg
slicer or with a stainless-steel knife. Add eggs to the sauce

and very gently stir them into the sauce with a two-pronged fork. Stir as little as possible and try not to break up the yolks. Heat thoroughly and serve on toast or with rice.

Yield: Two to four servings.

CURRIED EGGS

¼ cup raisins (optional)
1½ tablespoons butter
3 tablespoons minced
    onion
3 tablespoons flour
1 teaspoon curry powder
¾ cup milk
¼ cup heavy cream

Salt and freshly ground
    pepper to taste
4 hard-cooked eggs
    (*see page 39*),
    thinly sliced
¼ cup toasted almonds
    (optional)
Chutney

1. If the raisins are to be used, place them in a small mixing bowl and add boiling water to cover. Let stand for 10 minutes and drain.

2. Melt the butter in a 3- or 4-cup saucepan and add the onion. Cook, stirring with a wire whisk, until onion is wilted. Do not brown. Sprinkle with the flour and curry powder and gradually add the milk, stirring rapidly with the whisk. When the mixture is thickened and smooth stir in the cream and add salt and pepper to taste.

3. Add the eggs and gradually and gently fold them into the sauce, using a rubber spatula. Do not overblend or break up the eggs. Heat thoroughly and serve on hot plates with rice. Serve with the drained raisins, which should now be plumped, the toasted almonds (if used), and the chutney.

Yield: Two to four servings.

CHEESE SAUCE FOR VEGETABLES

This is a very simple and very good recipe for a thin cheese sauce to be served over vegetables.

1 tablespoon butter
1 tablespoon flour
1 cup milk (or use ¾ cup milk and ¼ cup heavy cream)
Salt and freshly ground pepper to taste
⅛ teaspoon nutmeg or to taste
⅛ teaspoon cayenne pepper or to taste
¾ cup grated sharp Cheddar cheese

1. Heat the butter in a 3- or 4-cup saucepan and when butter is melted add the flour. Stir with a wire whisk and when blended add the liquid, stirring vigorously and constantly. Add the salt, pepper, nutmeg, and cayenne.
2. Cook, stirring occasionally, for about 5 minutes or longer.
3. Remove the sauce from the heat and stir in the grated cheese. Serve hot over cooked cauliflower, asparagus, or other suitable vegetables.
Yield: About 1 cup.

SAUCE MORNAY

3 tablespoons butter
3 tablespoons flour
1¾ cups milk
¼ cup heavy cream
Salt and freshly ground pepper to taste
¼ teaspoon nutmeg
⅛ teaspoon cayenne pepper
1½ cups grated Cheddar, Gruyère, or Swiss cheese
1 teaspoon Worcestershire sauce (optional)

1. Melt the butter in a 6-cup saucepan over medium heat and add the flour. Stir with a wire whisk until blended.

2. Add the milk and cream, stirring rapidly with the whisk, and bring to a boil. When thickened and smooth add the salt, pepper, nutmeg, and cayenne and let simmer, stirring occasionally.

3. Remove the sauce from the heat and stir in the cheese. Add the Worcestershire sauce and keep warm. This sauce may be served on toast or with poached eggs as in the recipe that follows.

Yield: About 3 cups.

DISHES TO MAKE FROM SAUCE MORNAY

EGGS MORNAY

8 slices buttered toast
4 thin slices ham, cooked
   in a skillet in a little
   butter until heated
   through
4 poached eggs
   (*see page 43*)

3 cups Mornay sauce
   (*see preceding*
   recipe)
Paprika or parsley sprigs
   for garnish

1. Cut 4 slices of the toast diagonally to make triangles. Place a whole slice of toast in the center of four hot plates. Arrange the toast triangles on either side of each square of toast. Top each square of toast with a slice of ham and then a poached egg.

2. Spoon the hot sauce over the eggs. Serve garnished with a sprinkle of paprika or a sprig of parsley.

Yield: Four servings.

CRAB MEAT MORNAY

4 tablespoons (½ stick)
butter
2 tablespoons flour
1 cup milk
½ cup grated Swiss,
Gruyère, or sharp
Cheddar cheese
¼ cup heavy cream
½ teaspoon salt or more
to taste
¼ teaspoon freshly
ground black pepper
⅛ teaspoon cayenne
pepper
½ teaspoon Worcester-
shire sauce
1 pound fresh or canned
crab meat
4 tablespoons grated
Parmesan cheese

1. Place the broiler rack about five inches from the source of heat. Heat the broiler.

2. Melt half the butter in a small saucepan and stir in the flour, using a wire whisk. Add the milk, stirring rapidly with the whisk. When the sauce is thickened and smooth, remove the saucepan from the heat and stir in the Swiss cheese. When the cheese melts, add the cream. Add the salt, black pepper, cayenne pepper, and Worcestershire sauce. Bring the sauce just to a boil and keep warm.

3. Pick over the crab meat to remove all bits of shell or cartilage.

4. Melt the remaining butter in a skillet and add the crab meat. Heat thoroughly but do not break up the crab meat. Spoon the crab meat into four or six small, oven-proof serving dishes, shells, or casseroles (ramekins) and then divide the sauce over the crab meat. Sprinkle with Parmesan cheese and arrange the filled dishes on a baking sheet. Place the dishes under the broiler until bubbly, hot, and lightly browned.

Yield: Four to six servings.

SHRIMP MORNAY

Substitute 1 pound of cooked, shelled, and deveined shrimp for the crab meat in the preceding recipe.

POACHED EGGS À LA JÉREZ (Eggs with Sherry-Flavored Mornay Sauce)

1½ tablespoons butter
1½ tablespoons flour
¾ cup milk
¼ cup heavy cream
Salt and freshly ground
    black pepper to taste
2 egg yolks, lightly beaten
    (save whites for other
    use)

½ cup grated Gruyère
    or Swiss cheese
3 tablespoons dry sherry
3 English muffins, pulled
    apart and toasted
12 slices crisp bacon
6 hot poached eggs
    (*see page 43*)
Paprika
Watercress for garnish

1. Melt the butter in a saucepan and stir in the flour with a wire whisk. When blended, add the milk and cream, stirring vigorously with the whisk. Continue stirring and cooking until the sauce thickens. Add salt and pepper and continue to simmer for 5 or 10 minutes longer.

2. Remove the sauce from the heat and stir in the yolks, beating rapidly. Add the cheese and when it melts stir in the sherry. Keep hot but do not boil or the excess heat will make the yolks curdle the sauce.

3. Place a toasted muffin half on each of six plates and top each with 2 strips of bacon. Add a poached egg to each plate and cover with the sauce. Sprinkle with paprika and garnish each plate with a few sprigs of watercress.

Yield: Six servings.

CELESTIAL CHICKEN IN VELVET SAUCE

This is one of the simplest of dishes to prepare and it is also one of the most delicious. It is heavy with cream and is not designed for people who worry about calories. This is precisely the way this dish would be prepared by a celebrated French chef. It is the recipe, in fact, of a celebrated French chef.

A 3½-pound chicken, cleaned and trussed with strings by the butcher
1 onion, peeled and studded with 1 clove
1 bay leaf
¼ teaspoon dried thyme or 2 sprigs fresh thyme
10 peppercorns
2 carrots, scraped and cut in half
2 ribs celery, washed and cut in half

1 clove garlic, peeled
Salt to taste
Water to cover
3 tablespoons butter
3 tablespoons flour
1 cup cream
1 egg yolk, slightly beaten (save white for other use)
1 tablespoon lemon juice
¼ teaspoon nutmeg, preferably freshly grated
Freshly ground black pepper to taste

1. Place the trussed chicken in a kettle large enough to hold it comfortably. If the kettle is too large it will take too much water to cook the chicken.

2. Add the onion, bay leaf, thyme, peppercorns, carrots, celery, garlic, salt, and water to cover. The water level should be about ½ inch over the top of the chicken. Do not cover but bring to a boil and let simmer for 45 minutes to 1 hour.

3. Transfer the chicken to a warm platter and untruss it. Cover the chicken with aluminum foil to keep it warm.

Strain the stock and put it back on the stove to boil until ready for use, 10 to 15 minutes. The stock will keep boiling and reducing and becoming more concentrated in flavor.

4. Melt the butter in a saucepan and stir in the flour, using a wire whisk. Add 1½ cups of the boiling chicken stock while stirring vigorously with the whisk. When the mixture is thickened and smooth, continue to simmer over low heat for 15 minutes. The remaining stock in the kettle may be refrigerated for another use, such as soup or the base for another sauce.

5. Add the cream to the sauce and stir well. Continue to cook for 15 minutes, stirring frequently with the whisk. Remove the sauce from the heat and add the yolk, stirring rapidly. Add the lemon juice and nutmeg. Season to taste with salt and pepper. Spoon a little of the sauce over the chicken and serve the rest separately. The ideal accompaniment for this dish is rice with bay leaf.

Yield: Four servings.

MACARONI AND CHEESE

½ pound (8 ounces) raw
   elbow macaroni
4 tablespoons (½ stick)
   butter
2 tablespoons flour
2 cups hot milk
Salt and freshly ground
   black pepper to taste

¼ teaspoon nutmeg
⅛ teaspoon cayenne
   pepper (optional)
2 cups diced sharp
   Cheddar cheese
2 tablespoons grated
   Parmesan cheese

1. Preheat the oven to 375 degrees.

2. Cook the macaroni according to package directions but be careful not to overcook it. It should be tender but not mushy. Pour the macaroni into a colander and im-

mediately rinse with cold water. This will keep the macaroni from sticking together. Set aside.

3. Melt half the butter and stir in the flour, using a wire
whisk. Add the milk, stirring rapidly with the whisk.
Bring to a boil, stirring constantly. When the mixture is
thickened and smooth, add salt, pepper, nutmeg, and cayenne pepper. Remove the saucepan from the heat and stir
in the Cheddar cheese.

4. Butter a 2-quart baking dish and pour a little of the
sauce over the bottom. Add a layer of macaroni, more
sauce, and so on, but end with a layer of sauce. Sprinkle
with Parmesan cheese and dot with remaining butter. Bake
until bubbling and golden-brown, about 25 minutes.

Yield: Four to six servings.

CREAMED CRAB MEAT

3 tablespoons butter
3 tablespoons flour
1 cup milk
1 cup cream
Salt to taste
½ teaspoon dry mustard
⅓ cup dry sherry
    (optional)
2 cups crab meat, picked
    over well to remove all
bits of shell and
    cartilage
2 tablespoons finely
    chopped onion
¾ cup chopped green
    pepper
1 tomato, thinly sliced
Freshly ground black
    pepper to taste
1 tablespoon grated
    Parmesan cheese

1. Preheat the oven to 350 degrees.

2. Melt 2 tablespoons of the butter in a saucepan and
stir in the flour, using a wire whisk. When blended, stir in
the milk and cream, stirring vigorously with the whisk.
Add the salt and mustard and bring to a boil, stirring.

When the mixture is blended and smooth, add the sherry. Simmer for 15 minutes.

3. Meanwhile, place the crab meat in a saucepan. Add the onion and green pepper and stir in half the sauce. Very gently stir to blend but do not break up the crab meat. Bring to a boil.

4. Spoon the hot crab-meat mixture into a pie plate or a similar flat ovenproof baking dish. Spoon the remaining sauce over the mixture. Neatly arrange the tomato slices over the top and sprinkle with salt, pepper, and Parmesan cheese. Dot with the remaining butter.

5. Bake just until mixture bubbles in the dish.

6. Place under the broiler just long enough to brown the cheese.

Yield: Six servings.

Variation: It is very easy to vary the flavors of dishes, and all that is essential is an iota of taste and imagination. For example, the preceding creamed crab meat could be curried. To do this, omit the sherry and add curry powder to taste along with the flour before making the sauce. You would not use both sherry and curry because it would be an unnecessary complication of flavors. On the other hand, you could also make substitutions for the crab meat. Flaked cooked fish such as tuna or salmon could be substituted, or even chopped hard-cooked eggs could be used.

SAUCE BELLE AURORE

It is not necessary to be a professional chef to produce some of the best sauces of classic French cookery. Here, for example, is a delicious sauce for ham or poached eggs. It is called *sauce belle aurore* (beautiful dawn) because of its rosy tint.

7 tablespoons butter
½ cup finely chopped
  onion
1 small clove garlic,
  finely minced
2 cups chopped fresh
  tomatoes or an equal
  amount of drained
  canned tomatoes (the
  fresh tomatoes need
  not be peeled)

¼ teaspoon thyme
1 small bay leaf
Salt and freshly ground
  pepper to taste
3 tablespoons flour
2½ cups fresh or canned
  chicken broth
1 cup heavy cream
¼ cup port wine

1. This sauce is made in two parts. For the first part, use a 1-quart saucepan. Heat 1 tablespoon of the butter in the saucepan and add the onion and garlic. Cook, stirring with a wooden spoon, over moderate heat until onion is wilted.

2. Add the tomatoes, thyme, and bay leaf. Season to taste with salt and pepper. Bring to a boil and simmer slowly for 15 minutes. Stir the sauce occasionally as it simmers.

3. While that sauce cooks, prepare the second sauce. Use a 2-quart saucepan and add 3 tablespoons of the remaining butter. Let it melt and then stir in the flour with a wire whisk. Stir until butter and flour are blended and

continue to stir rapidly while adding the chicken stock. The mixture, when it boils, should be thick and smooth. Simmer, stirring occasionally, until the tomato sauce is ready.

4. Stir the tomato sauce into the second sauce and continue cooking about ½ hour. Add the cup of heavy cream and bring to a boil. Pour the sauce through a strainer and bring once more to a boil. Remove the sauce from the heat and swirl in the remaining 3 tablespoons of butter. Add the wine. Bring the sauce just to a boil but do not boil. Serve with poached eggs or hot sliced boiled ham.

Yield: About 4 cups.

SAUCE FOR BOILED BEEF

The following recipe for sauce for boiled beef is made with I tablespoon of flour for each cup of liquid; thus it is a thin sauce.

1 tablespoon butter	Salt and freshly ground
1 tablespoon flour	black pepper to taste
1 cup beef broth	

1. Heat the butter in a 3- or 4-cup saucepan and when butter is melted add the flour. Stir with a wire whisk and when blended add the broth, stirring vigorously and constantly.

2. Cook, stirring occasionally, for about 5 minutes or longer. Season to taste with salt and pepper and serve with hot boiled beef.

Yield: About 1 cup.

CAPER SAUCE FOR BOILED BEEF

Add 2 tablespoons or more of drained, bottled capers to the sauce for boiled beef just before serving.

HORSERADISH SAUCE FOR BOILED BEEF

Add 1 tablespoon or more of horseradish to the sauce for boiled beef just before serving. If possible, use freshly grated rather than bottled horseradish. If bottled horseradish is used, place it in a clean, small square of cloth or in paper toweling and squeeze to extract most of the moisture. As indicated above, add it according to taste.

The Oil and Butter Sauces

NEXT TO THE WHITE SAUCE given in the preceding chapter, the three most important sauces in the art of cooking are mayonnaise, hollandaise, and *béarnaise*. Mayonnaise has a thousand variations as the base for other dressings and, of course, as a spread for sandwiches. Hollandaise is used for cooked vegetables, boiled fish and meats. It is one of the most delicate and one of the richest of sauces. *Béarnaise* is a savory cousin, spiced with tarragon vinegar and shallots, and it is used for broiled meats, grilled fish, and the like.

Mayonnaise is a sauce based on eggs and oil.

Hollandaise and *béarnaise* are both based on eggs and butter.

MAYONNAISE

Homemade mayonnaise tastes much better than any that is sold commercially. It is easy to make using a wire whisk, electric mixer, or rotary beater, but the steps outlined below should be followed closely.

1 egg yolk (save white for another purpose)	¼ teaspoon dry mustard
Salt and freshly ground black pepper to taste	2 teaspoons or more vinegar or lemon juice
⅛ teaspoon cayenne pepper	¾ to 1 cup peanut oil, salad oil, or olive oil

1. Place the yolk in a mixing bowl and add the salt, pepper, cayenne, and mustard.

2. Add the vinegar or lemon juice and start beating with a wire whisk, rotary beater, or electric mixer. Do not stop beating until the mayonnaise is made.

3. Start adding the oil in a very thin stream or drop by drop. When half the oil has been added, the rest may be added in a larger stream. Taste the mayonnaise and, if desired, add more vinegar or salt to taste. Now this is important. Homemade mayonnaise should be stabilized when it is to be stored, if it has been freshly made. To do this

beat in a little water, about 1 teaspoon at a time. Do not make it too thin. Use your judgment. One cup of mayonnaise may take about 2 teaspoons of water. Of course, if you want a thin mayonnaise to use as a sauce you may add more but it is not necessary for stability in the refrigerator.

Yield: About 1 cup.

Tips on Making Mayonnaise

☞ If the mayonnaise curdles as it is being made, there are several ways to "bring it back":

Start with a fresh egg yolk and beat in the curdled mixture plus an additional cup of oil to compensate for the extra yolk.

Or, add a little ice water or a small sliver of ice to a clean, cold mixing bowl and start beating while adding the curdled mixture.

Or, place a tablespoon of already made mayonnaise in a mixing bowl and start beating in the curdled mixture.

☞ A mayonnaise made exclusively with olive oil is generally too strong for most palates. Half peanut oil and half olive oil is a good compromise.

☞ The mayonnaise may be spooned into a jar or small mixing bowl. Covered tightly, the mayonnaise will keep for more than a week in the refrigerator.

BLENDER MAYONNAISE

Mayonnaise may be made in a blender, in which case the whole egg may be used. There is nothing tricky about this if the steps outlined below are closely followed. There is essentially no difference in the texture of the mayonnaise made by hand and that made in the blender. Hand-made mayonnaise, which contains only yolks, may be preferable to blender mayonnaise made with whole egg, but it is a question of taste.

1 whole egg
½ teaspoon dry mustard
½ teaspoon salt
2 tablespoons vinegar or
    lemon juice

1 cup peanut oil, salad
    oil, olive oil, or a
    combination

1. To the container of an electric blender add the egg, mustard, salt, vinegar, and *exactly* ¼ cup of oil.
2. Cover and turn the motor on low speed. Quickly uncover and add the remaining oil in a steady stream. When the mayonnaise is made, spoon it into a small mixing bowl or jar for storage in the refrigerator. Now this is important. Homemade mayonnaise should be stabilized when it is to be stored, if it has been freshly made. To do this beat in a little water, about 1 teaspoon at a time. Do not make it too thin. Use your judgment. One cup of mayonnaise may take about 2 teaspoons of water. Of course, if you want a thin mayonnaise to use as a sauce you may add more but it is not necessary for stability in the refrigerator.

Yield: About 1¼ cups.

THE MAYONNAISE VARIATIONS

TARTARE SAUCE

1 cup mayonnaise
2 tablespoons finely chopped sour pickles (preferably imported, the ones known in France as *cornichons*)
3 tablespoons finely minced capers
1 tablespoon finely chopped fresh parsley
1 tablespoon finely chopped fresh chives or green onion
½ tablespoon finely chopped fresh tarragon or 1 teaspoon dried tarragon

Combine all the ingredients and chill. Serve with cold fish and seafood, such as salmon, crab, and shrimp, and with deep-fried fish or seafood.

SAUCE GRIBICHE

Prepare the preceding tartare sauce and add a finely chopped hard-cooked egg. Serve with poached fish, seafood, calf's head, or cold meats.

MAYONNAISE SALADS

In the world of food there are many threads of similarity between one category of cooking and another. For example, in making creamed dishes the general rule is to use two cups of cooked solids such as meat, fish, poultry, or whatever to one cup of cream sauce. The same rule applies to the various mayonnaise salads. For each two cups of food such as cubed shrimp, crab, chicken, or whatever, use one cup of mayonnaise. A typical mayonnaise-salad recipe follows.

SEAFOOD SALAD

2 cups cooked shrimp, crab, or lobster, cut into bite-sized cubes
1 cup mayonnaise
1 tablespoon finely minced parsley
½ cup finely diced heart of celery
1 teaspoon finely minced onion, chives, or scallions (green onions)
Salt and freshly ground black pepper to taste
Lemon juice to taste
Lettuce leaves

1. Place the seafood in a 3- or 4-cup mixing bowl and add the mayonnaise.
2. Add the parsley, celery, onion, salt, pepper, and lemon

juice and toss lightly until all pieces of seafood are coated.
Serve on lettuce leaves.

Yield: Two to four servings.

Variations: Replace the seafood in the recipe with cubes
of cooked, boneless, skinless chicken.

Or add a tablespoon of drained capers to the ingredients
before tossing.

Or season to taste with a few drops of Tabasco and/or
Worcestershire sauce before tossing.

LOUIS DRESSING

1 cup mayonnaise
¼ cup heavy cream
¼ cup chili sauce
3 tablespoons finely
     minced green pepper
3 tablespoons finely
     chopped chives or
     scallions (green
     onions; use the green
     part and all)

2 tablespoons finely
     chopped stuffed green
     olives
½ teaspoon Worcester-
     shire sauce
Salt and freshly ground
     black pepper to taste
Lemon juice to taste

Combine all ingredients and chill. Serve with cold seafood, particularly crab.

Yield: About 1¾ cups.

CRAB LOUIS

1 pound lump crab meat
     or, if unavailable,
     canned crab meat
Lettuce leaves
¾ cup Louis dressing
     (*see preceding recipe*)

4 hard-cooked eggs
     (*see page 39*)
2 small tomatoes,
     quartered
4 or more large stuffed
     green olives

1. Pick over the crab meat, if necessary, to remove bits of cartilage and shell.

2. Arrange lettuce leaves on four chilled plates and add equal portions of crab on each. Spoon the dressing over the crab.

3. Garnish the plates with hard-cooked eggs, tomatoes, and stuffed olives and serve.

Yield: Four servings.

HOLLANDAISE SAUCE

It is a mystery why so many people regard the making of a hollandaise with awe and apprehension. It is one of the easiest sauces to make if you know the basic techniques. Most manuals seem to complicate the process by directing that unmelted butter be added bit by bit and sometimes alternately with water and seasonings.

Follow these steps explicitly and the best hollandaise conceivable will result. It is important to have a wire whisk and a saucepan with a fairly heavy bottom. To start the recipe, this saucepan is placed in a skillet that contains simmering water. A double boiler may be used, but it is more confining. In any event, DO NOT USE AN ALUMINUM SAUCEPAN, because the sauce will darken.

The ingredients for a perfect hollandaise are:

12 tablespoons (¾ cup; 1½ sticks) butter
3 egg yolks (save whites for another purpose)
2 tablespoons cold water

Salt to taste
1 teaspoon lemon juice
⅛ teaspoon cayenne pepper

1. Place a skillet on the stove and add about ½ inch of water. Bring this water to the simmering point—that is, until it bubbles gently.

2. Place the butter in a small saucepan and let butter

melt over low heat. Do not let the butter bubble, just melt it.

3. Select a 1½- or 2-quart saucepan and set it in the simmering water.

4. Add the 3 egg yolks to the saucepan and then 2 tablespoons of cold water. Now comes the critical part of this recipe. You must start beating the eggs with a wire whisk and beat them well. Let the whisk move briskly all around the saucepan, back and forth and in a circular motion. Continue beating until the eggs become frothy and slightly thickened. The eggs when ready will be yellow and custard-like and still somewhat frothy. This will take only 1 or 2 minutes.

5. Immediately remove the saucepan from the skillet and place the saucepan on a table. Start adding the melted butter while beating vigorously with the whisk, back and forth and in a circular motion. Continue beating until all the butter is added. Add salt to taste, lemon juice, and cayenne pepper and beat. The sauce may be heated very gently by returning the saucepan to the skillet, but the sauce must be stirred constantly with the whisk.

Yield: About 1 cup.

BLENDER HOLLANDAISE

16 tablespoons (1 cup;
  2 sticks) butter
4 egg yolks (save whites
  for another purpose)

2 tablespoons lemon juice
Salt to taste
⅛ teaspoon cayenne
  pepper

1. Melt the butter in a saucepan over low heat. Heat butter to bubbling but do not let it brown.

2. Meanwhile, into the container of an electric blender add the remaining ingredients. Cover the container and blend on low speed. The yolks must not be overblended or the sauce will not make. Immediately uncover and pour in the hot butter in a steady stream. When all butter is incorporated, turn off motor. Keep the sauce warm by placing the container in a saucepan with two inches of hot water. If the sauce becomes too thick, thin it with a little hot water briefly blended.

Yield: 1¼ cups.

SAUCE MOUSSELINE

This is hollandaise with whipped cream. To prepare the sauce, spoon 1 cup of freshly made hollandaise into a warm serving bowl and spoon over it ½ cup of whipped cream (¼ cup heavy cream whipped will yield ½ cup) seasoned with a judicious amount of salt. The uses for *sauce mousseline* are the same as for hollandaise.

SAUCE MALTAISE (Orange-Flavored Hollandaise)

This is good served with cooked asparagus, broccoli, beets, or carrots. Stir 1 tablespoon of orange juice and 2 teaspoons of grated orange rind into 1 cup of hollandaise.

BÉARNAISE SAUCE

This herbal cousin of hollandaise was named after the birth-place of Henri IV, Béarn, an historic, former French province in Southwest France. The principal herb and flavor of the sauce is tarragon.

12 tablespoons (¾ cup;
    1½ sticks) butter
3 tablespoons tarragon
    vinegar
1 tablespoon finely
    chopped shallot or
    onion
1 tablespoon chopped
    fresh tarragon or half
    the amount dried

3 egg yolks (save whites
    for another purpose)
2 tablespoons cold water
Salt to taste
1 teaspoon lemon juice
⅛ teaspoon cayenne
    pepper
1½ tablespoons freshly
    chopped tarragon
    leaves or half the
    amount dried

1. Place a skillet on the stove and add about ½ inch of water. Bring this water to the simmering point—that is, until it bubbles gently.

2. Place the butter in a small saucepan and let butter melt over low heat. Do not let the butter bubble; just melt it.

3. Select a 1½- or 2-quart heavy saucepan and add the vinegar, shallots, and 1 tablespoon chopped tarragon. Place over direct heat and cook slowly until most of the vinegar evaporates. Remove the saucepan from the heat and let stand until cool.

4. Set the saucepan in the simmering water.

5. Add the 3 egg yolks to the saucepan and then 2 table-spoons of cold water. Now comes the critical part of this recipe. You must start by beating the egg yolks with a wire whisk and beat them well. Let the whisk move briskly all

around the saucepan, back and forth and in a circular motion. Continue beating until the eggs become frothy and slightly thickened. The eggs when ready will be yellow and custard-like and still somewhat frothy. This will require only 1 or 2 minutes.

6. Immediately remove the saucepan from the skillet and place saucepan on the table. Start adding the melted butter while beating vigorously with the whisk, back and forth and in a circular motion. Continue beating until all the butter is added. Add salt to taste, lemon juice, cayenne pepper, and the chopped tarragon leaves and beat. The sauce may be heated very gently by returning the saucepan to the skillet, but the sauce must be stirred constantly with the whisk.

Yield: About 1 cup.

NOTE: *Béarnaise* sauce is used for grilled and broiled meats and fish.

BLENDER BÉARNAISE

1¼ cups blender hollan-
daise (*see page 89*)
2 tablespoons tarragon
vinegar
2 tablespoons dry white
wine

1 tablespoon chopped
fresh tarragon or half
the amount dried
1 tablespoon chopped
shallot or green
onion (scallion)

1. Prepare the hollandaise according to the directions on page 89.
2. Combine the remaining ingredients in a small sauce-pan and cook until almost all the liquid evaporates. Spoon what remains into the hollandaise and blend on high speed for 6 seconds.

Yield: About 1¼ cups.

THE BASIC FRENCH DRESSING

The French, the sauce masters, call this *sauce salade*. The basic recipe is made solely with oil, vinegar, salt, and pepper, but there are hundreds of variations. However, French dressing should always be freshly made, and if it contains garlic and spices it should not be allowed to stand in the refrigerator for more than an hour or so. The dressing loses its fresh quality, which is essential for good salads.

½ to 1 tablespoon wine
vinegar (the amount
will depend on the
strength of the
vinegar)
½ teaspoon salt

Freshly ground black
pepper to taste
3 tablespoons peanut oil,
salad oil, or olive oil,
or a combination

Place the vinegar, salt, and pepper in a salad bowl or mixing bowl and add the oil while beating with a wire whisk.

Yield: About ¼ cup, enough for a salad for two.

VARIATIONS

1. Lemon juice may be substituted for part or all of the vinegar.

2. All olive oil in this dressing may be too strong for some palates. If it is used, it is best to combine it with another oil. Most French chefs rarely use all olive oil in this dressing. They use peanut oil, vegetable oil, or one of these oils with a little olive oil.

AN EXCELLENT VERSION OF FRENCH DRESSING

½ clove garlic
Salt
½ to 1 tablespoon wine
 vinegar
½ teaspoon prepared
 mustard, preferably
 Düsseldorf or Dijon
available in this coun-
try (*see note below*)
2 drops Tabasco sauce
3 tablespoons peanut oil,
 olive oil, or a com-
 bination of both

Chop the garlic with the salt until it is almost a paste and add it to a salad bowl or mixing bowl. Stir in the remaining ingredients, using a wire whisk, until well blended.

Yield: About ¼ cup, enough for a salad for two.

NOTE: Düsseldorf or Dijon mustard is stressed here because it is superior to many prepared mustards made in this country. By all means do not use what could be called "baseball-lot mustard" in this recipe.

VINAIGRETTE SAUCE

3 tablespoons wine
    vinegar
¾ cup olive oil
½ cup chopped parsley
1 tablespoon capers,
    chopped and drained
1 teaspoon finely chopped
    onion

1 teaspoon finely chopped
    sour pickle
Salt and freshly ground
    black pepper to taste
1 hard-cooked egg,
    chopped

1. Combine all the ingredients and beat with a fork until well blended.

2. Heat sauce to lukewarm to serve with hot boiled beef. The sauce may be served cold with cold shrimp or crab meat.

Yield: About 1¼ cups sauce.

A basic sauce made with tomatoes is one of the most versatile in the entire range of cooking. Tomato sauce has a thousand different uses in the Italian repertory, and its uses on the local scene are seemingly without limit. It is good on any pasta such as spaghetti or linguine, with croquettes, and the tomato sauce that follows is particularly good with meat loaves.

The thing to remember about a tomato sauce is that the flavor of the tomatoes used in making it is all-important. If the tomatoes are succulent and full of flavor, the sauce is apt to be also. If canned tomatoes are to be used for this sauce, buy those marked "Italian peeled" or "Italian plum," for they are the best.

Many herbs, such as parsley, thyme, and tarragon, go well with tomatoes, but the one that complements tomatoes best is basil. Some brands of canned tomatoes are packed with basil.

Tomato paste is frequently called for in tomato sauces for two basic reasons: primarily because it gives body to a sauce and tends to thicken it, but also because it adds color. But the paste should be used with discretion because it is rather strong in flavor.

NOTE: To peel tomatoes easily, spear them one at a time at the stem end with a two-pronged fork. Dip them into a saucepan of boiling fresh water and let them stand, completely immersed in the water, for exactly 12 seconds. Withdraw them immediately and use a sharp paring knife to pull off the skin. The skins slip off easily.

TOMATO SAUCE I

2 cups chopped onion (2 to 3 medium onions)
1 clove garlic, finely minced
2 tablespoons olive oil
4 large red, ripe tomatoes, cored, peeled (*see note*), and chopped, or 4 cups canned plum tomatoes (2-pound-3-ounce can)

3 tablespoons tomato paste
1 cup beef broth or water
¼ cup finely chopped parsley
1 or 2 sprigs fresh basil or 1 teaspoon dried basil
2 sprigs fresh thyme or ¼ teaspoon dried thyme
Salt and freshly ground black pepper to taste
½ teaspoon sugar

1. Use a medium-sized saucepan or casserole with heavy

bottom. Cook the onion and garlic in the olive oil until the onion is wilted.

2. It is not essential but it is preferable if tomatoes are put through a food mill before adding to the sauce to remove the seeds. The seeds do add a slightly bitter taste.

3. Pour the tomatoes into a saucepan, add the remaining ingredients, and bring to a boil. Simmer, stirring frequently, for about 45 minutes. If the sauce is not stirred frequently it may stick to the bottom and scorch. When the sauce

has cooked for 45 minutes it is suitable for serving. Some cooks prefer a smoother sauce. To prepare one, put the sauce through a food mill and return it to the saucepan. Simmer, stirring frequently, for 15 minutes more. If desired, add more salt and pepper to taste.

Yield: About 5 cups.

NOTE: Any leftover sauce may be frozen for future use.

TOMATO SAUCE II

3 tablespoons olive oil
2 tablespoons butter
1 cup finely chopped
  onion (about 1½
  medium onions)
1 clove garlic, finely minced
½ cup chopped, seeded, and
  cored green pepper
2 cups Italian peeled
  tomatoes (1-pound-1-
  ounce can)

Salt and freshly ground
  black pepper to taste
¼ teaspoon or more sugar
2 tablespoons chopped fresh
  basil or ½ teaspoon
  dried basil
1 sprig fresh thyme or ½
  teaspoon dried thyme
1 bay leaf
2 tablespoons tomato paste
½ cup beef stock or water

1. Heat 2 tablespoons of the oil and the butter in a heavy casserole and cook the onion, garlic, and chopped pepper until onion is wilted but not brown.

2. It is not essential but it is preferable if the tomatoes are put through a food mill before adding to the sauce to remove the seeds. The seeds do add a slightly bitter taste.

3. Add the tomatoes, salt, pepper, sugar, basil, thyme, bay leaf, tomato paste, and beef stock and stir well. Simmer over low heat for about 45 minutes, stirring occasionally. Sugar in this recipe should be added to taste.

4. Add the remaining tablespoon of oil and stir just until it is incorporated in the sauce. Remove the bay leaf and serve.

Yield: About 3 cups.

NOTE: This sauce may be put through a food mill if a smoother sauce is desired, then reheated, before serving. The sauce will keep for several days in the refrigerator and may be frozen.

TOMATO SAUCE III

3 tablespoons butter or
    salad oil
1 clove garlic, finely minced
½ cup chopped onion
    (about 1 small onion)
2 cups Italian plum toma-
    toes (1-pound-1-ounce
    can)

3 tablespoons tomato paste
½ cup beef broth, chicken
    stock, or water
½ to 1 teaspoon sugar
Salt and freshly ground
    black pepper to taste

1. Heat the butter or oil in a saucepan and add the garlic and onion. Cook, stirring occasionally with a wooden spoon, until the onion is wilted.

2. Add the tomatoes and cook, stirring occasionally, for 15 minutes. Add the tomato paste, liquid, sugar, salt, and pepper and continue cooking, stirring occasionally, for about 15 minutes more.

Yield: About 2½ cups.

TOMATO SAUCE VARIATIONS

Tomato sauce with mushrooms. After the onion and garlic have been cooked, add 1 cup of sliced mushrooms and cook, stirring, for about 5 minutes. Add the tomatoes and continue with the master recipe.

Tomato sauce with sausages. Broil 4 sweet or hot Italian sausages until done. Add them to the tomato sauce for the last 15 minutes of cooking.

Hot tomato sauce. Add ¼ teaspoon or more hot-pepper flakes to the tomato sauce.

A rich tomato sauce. Swirl 2 tablespoons of butter or olive oil into the sauce when it is finished.

Tomato sauce with horseradish. Horseradish may be added to taste to a tomato sauce that is to accompany a meat loaf, grilled pork chops, and the like. It would not be suitable for spaghetti.

Soups

ALTHOUGH HOMEMADE SOUPS are frequently neglected on to-day's menus, they are keenly appreciated whenever they appear at table. There is nothing, perhaps, more elegant for a well-planned dinner than a clear consommé or a cream soup, the choice of which would depend on the course to follow. A clear soup should precede a meal that might include a cream sauce. A cream soup should never precede a meal that includes a cream sauce; but it would be ideal before a roast, chicken, beef, steak, or the like.

There are basically three kinds of soups—these are the clear soups, cream soups, and vegetable soups. Clear soups are made with fish, poultry, or meat cooked in a broth and strained. Cream soups are nothing more than diluted white sauces to which cream and various flavors are added. Vegetable soups are peasant soups and are altogether delicious; they can be a meal in themselves.

In preparing the so-called clear soups or broths, it is important to know that bones give body to the liquids. What the body really is, is a form of gelatin. Veal bones give off the most gela-tin and, therefore, give the most body to soups and broths. The reason we say "so-called clear soups or broths" is that they are not transparent and water-clear when they are first made. A basic chicken soup or beef soup—otherwise known as stock— is delicious when it is served immediately out of the kettle. But if it is to be really clear, it must be "refined" with egg white or raw meat. This is a refinement, however, that few people in this day and age care to indulge in; it simply looks more elegant but is necessary only if the soup is used for an aspic, which must be clear. There are listed below recipes for a chicken stock and a beef stock, either of which may be served as a soup or as a cooking broth.

BEEF SOUP OR BROTH

2 pounds shin of beef
2-pound veal knuckle
Water
1½ tablespoons salt
1 onion, peeled and studded
   with 4 cloves
12 peppercorns
2 carrots, scraped and
   coarsely chopped

6 sprigs parsley
½ teaspoon thyme
1 bay leaf
2 ribs celery, coarsely
   chopped
1 white turnip, peeled and
   quartered, if available

1. Place the beef shin and the veal knuckle in a large saucepan or kettle and add cold water to cover. Bring to a boil and simmer for 5 minutes. Drain and discard the liquid.

2. Add 9 cups fresh cold water to the bones in the kettle and add all the remaining ingredients. Bring to a boil over moderate heat. Simmer uncovered for 2 hours. Using a large kitchen spoon, from time to time skim all the foam and scum that rises to the top of the soup as it boils, rinsing the spoon occasionally between skimmings.

3. Place a sieve over a large mixing bowl and line it with a piece of cheesecloth that has been rinsed in cold water. Very carefully pour the soup into the sieve so that it is strained into the bowl. Discard all the solid matter such as the bones, skin, vegetables, and spices. The meat could be used in any recipe calling for leftover beef or for sandwiches, salads, and so forth.

4. The resulting broth is now ready to be used. It may be served hot as a soup or the broth might be used to make other soups and sauces. Before serving or using the broth, however, you should taste it to make certain it has enough salt. Or you may wish a more concentrated soup, in which case you should not add more salt, but pour the liquid into a saucepan and cook it over high heat, skimming the surface once more, until it is reduced as much as you wish it. Remember that the more you cook the broth the richer it will become. If the soup is reduced this way, add the salt only at the end.

Yield: 4 to 6 cups of soup or broth.

CHICKEN SOUP OR BROTH

3 pounds bony chicken
    parts such as wings,
    necks, and backs
1 bay leaf
½ teaspoon thyme
12 peppercorns
2 ribs celery with leaves
1 large onion, peeled and
    studded with 2 cloves
1 carrot, scraped and
    coarsely chopped
6 sprigs parsley
10 cups water
1 tablespoon salt

1. Rinse the chicken pieces and place them in a large saucepan or kettle that will hold at least 4 quarts. Add the remaining ingredients and bring them to a boil over moderate heat. Simmer uncovered for 2 hours. Using a large kitchen spoon, skim from time to time all the scum and foam that rises to the top of the soup as it boils, rinsing the spoon occasionally between skimmings.

2. Place a sieve over a large mixing bowl and line it with a piece of cheesecloth that has been rinsed in cold water. Very carefully pour the soup into the sieve so that it is strained into the bowl. Discard all the solid matter such as the bones, skin, meat, vegetables, and spices.

3. The resulting broth is now ready to be used. It may be served hot as a soup or the broth might be used to make other soups and sauces. Before serving or using the broth, however, you should taste it to make certain it has enough salt. Or you may wish a more concentrated soup, in which case you should not add more salt but pour the liquid into a saucepan and cook it over high heat, skimming the surface once more, until it is reduced as much as you wish it. Remember that the more you cook the broth the richer it will become. If the soup is reduced this way, add the salt only at the end.

Yield: 4 to 6 cups of soup or broth.

TO CLEAR A SOUP WITH MEAT AND EGG WHITE

½ pound ground raw stewing meat
1 carrot, scraped and coarsely chopped
1 rib celery, without leaves, coarsely chopped
1 egg white (save yolk for another purpose)

4 cups cold beef or chicken soup
2 sprigs parsley
1 bay leaf
1 eggshell

1. Place the raw meat in a large saucepan and add the chopped carrot and celery. Blend lightly.

2. Beat the egg white lightly with a rotary beater or wire whisk. Do not beat until stiff, only frothy. Stir the egg white into the raw-meat mixture with a wooden spoon. Pour the cold broth over the meat and stir lightly with the spoon. Add the parsley and bay leaf. Crush the eggshell and add it.

3. Bring the mixture to a rolling boil, stirring constantly with a wooden spoon. Remove the saucepan from the heat.

4. Place a sieve over a mixing bowl and line it with a double layer of cheesecloth or with a piece of clean flannel. Pour the contents of the saucepan into the sieve and let it drain thoroughly. Reheat the broth before serving.

Yield: About 4 cups.

A BASIC CREAM SOUP

5 tablespoons butter
3 tablespoons flour
2 cups fresh or canned chicken broth
2 cups finely shredded lettuce, escarole, romaine, or spinach (*see note below*)
1 cup heavy cream
Salt and freshly ground black pepper to taste

1. Melt 3 tablespoons of the butter in a saucepan and stir in the flour, using a wire whisk.

2. Add the chicken broth, stirring vigorously with the whisk. When the mixture is thickened and smooth continue cooking over low heat for 15 minutes.

3. Stir in the shredded greens and the cream and simmer for 5 minutes more. Season the soup to taste with salt and pepper and turn off the heat. Stir in the remaining butter and when it melts serve the soup immediately in hot cups or soup plates.

Yield: Four to six servings.

NOTE: You could replace these greens with a cup of any puréed cooked vegetable, such as carrots, cauliflower, or asparagus.

CREAM OF WATERCRESS SOUP

2 cups fresh or canned
   chicken stock
20 tender watercress stems
3 tablespoons cornstarch
1 cup heavy cream

Salt and freshly ground
   black pepper to taste
1 teaspoon lemon juice
2 tablespoons cold butter
¾ cup loosely packed
   watercress leaves

1. Reserve ½ cup of the chicken stock. Place the remainder in a saucepan or casserole and add the watercress stems. Bring to a boil and simmer for about 5 minutes.

2. Blend the cornstarch with the reserved cold chicken stock and stir it into the boiling broth. Remove from the heat and blend in an electric blender. Add the cream and bring to a boil. Add salt and pepper to taste. Add the lemon juice and remove from the heat.

3. Swirl in the cold butter and add the watercress leaves. Serve immediately.

Yield: Four servings.

OYSTER STEW

4 tablespoons (½ stick)
   butter
1 onion, finely minced
½ cup finely minced celery
2 cups milk
2 cups heavy cream
2 cups shucked oysters
   (purchased in a pint
   container)

¼ teaspoon cayenne
   pepper
1 teaspoon Worcestershire
   sauce, or to taste
Salt and freshly ground
   black pepper to taste
Celery salt (optional)

1. Heat the butter in a 2-quart saucepan and cook the onion and celery until onion is translucent. Add the milk and cream and bring barely to a boil.

2. Add the undrained oysters and return just to a boil. When the oysters start to curl at the edges, which they should do almost immediately, remove the stew from the heat. Add the cayenne pepper, Worcestershire sauce, salt, and pepper and serve at once in hot plates. Add a dash of celery salt, if desired, to each serving. Serve with hot buttered toast.

Yield: Four servings.

ONION SOUP GRATINÉE

2 large Bermuda onions
4 tablespoons (½ stick) butter
1 clove garlic, finely minced
Salt and coarsely ground black pepper to taste
1 tablespoon flour

4 cups fresh or canned beef broth
2 cups water
½ teaspoon thyme
¼ bay leaf
12 thin slices French or Italian bread
½ cup grated Gruyère or Swiss cheese

1. Peel the onions and slice them almost wafer-thin.

2. Heat the butter in a large saucepan or small kettle and add the onions and garlic. Add the salt and pepper and cook, stirring, over low heat until onions are golden-brown. Do not burn.

3. Sprinkle the onions with the flour and continue cooking and stirring for 3 or 4 minutes more. Add the broth, water, thyme, and piece of bay leaf and bring to the boil. Simmer for ½ hour or more.

4. Meanwhile, preheat the oven to 500 degrees. Place the bread on a baking sheet and bake, turning the slices once, so that they brown well and evenly.

5. Turn the soup into a 1½-quart heatproof casserole. Float the toast on top and sprinkle with cheese. Place the

casserole in a baking dish to catch the drippings. Bake until soup is steaming hot and the cheese melted and golden.

Yield: Six or more servings.

FROM PEASANT STOCK TO A DISH FOR KINGS: LEEK AND POTATO SOUP

One of the easiest soups to make and certainly one of the most delicious is basically a peasant soup from France. It is made with leeks and potatoes. The soup is interesting because it illustrates several facets of cooking. By adding cream to the basic leek and potato stock, the soup becomes more sophisticated. If the soup is puréed before the cream is added, it is elegant served hot or cold and goes by the well-known name of *vichyssoise*. Please note that the proper pronunciation for the soup is "veeshee-swahz," not "veeshee-swah" as too many people have it. The basic soup and variations are given here.

2 large leeks
1 medium-sized onion, finely chopped (about ¾ cup)
3 tablespoons butter
2 medium-sized potatoes, peeled and cut into cubes (about 2 cups)
3 cups chicken broth
Salt to taste, if necessary
Freshly ground black pepper to taste

1. Leeks are the most delicate member of the onion family. They rather resemble giant-sized spring onions or scallions as they are called. Leeks have a great deal of sand between their leaves and must be carefully cleaned. To do this, trim off the root end. Cut off and discard half of the long green stems. Slit the leeks lengthwise from the stem end, then turn and slit them once more. Rinse well, sepa-

rating the leaves, under cold running water. Shake them well, then chop them into small cubes.

2. Cook the chopped leeks and the onion in butter, stirring frequently, for about 5 minutes. Do not brown. Add the potatoes and chicken broth and bring to a boil. Simmer until the cubed potatoes are delicately tender, about 15 minutes. Season if necessary with salt, add the pepper, and serve hot.

Yield: Four servings.

LEEK AND POTATO SOUP WITH CREAM

Leek and potato soup is, as noted, a very good and basic peasant dish (originally made, by the way, with water instead of chicken stock). To glorify the same dish one need only add 1 cup heavy cream, bring just to a boil, and taste for seasoning. If necessary, add salt and pepper. Serve hot, sprinkled with chopped chives.

VICHYSSOISE

Prepare the original leek and potato soup. Pour the soup into a food mill or electric blender and purée it. (A food mill is preferable because the blender gives a thinner texture.) Return the soup to the saucepan in which it cooked and add 1 cup heavy cream. Add a drop or two of Tabasco sauce and, if desired, a dash of Worcestershire sauce (even some French chefs add it). Serve the soup in cups, either piping hot or very cold. However it is served, add a sprinkle of chopped chives as a garnish.

Variations: A pinch of saffron added to the original leek and potato soup along with the potatoes gives a Spanish dash to the soup. The saffron also gives a very pleasant yellow color.

Vichyssoise can be turned into something called *soupe MacIlwane* by adding small cubes of tomato and chopped green onion as a garnish rather than the chopped chives.

Tiny cubes of cucumber, well chilled, are good as a garnish for cold *vichyssoise*.

ENTRÉES AND/OR MAIN-COURSE DISHES

How to Buy Fresh Fish and Shellfish . . . Examples
of Shrimp and Lobster Cooked to Perfection . . .
Poaching, Cooking Meunière-Style, and Broiling
Fish . . . How to Purchase and Store Meat and
Poultry . . . Fundamentals of Beef Cookery, of Lamb,
of Veal, of Pork, and of Poultry with Recipes for
Roasting, Stewing, Grilling, and Frying Same . . . Cooking
Timetables and Rules for Fat Removal

Fish and Shellfish

THE ESSENTIAL THING to look for in purchasing fish or shellfish is freshness. Smell is the best clue to freshness. If the fish smells clean and pure, chances are it is fresh. If it smells high, discard or otherwise shun it.

In addition, freshness in a fish is determined by the color of the eyes and the gills. The eyes should be crystal clear or nearly so and the gills should be bright red.

Here are several basic recipes for fish and shellfish.

PLAIN BOILED SHRIMP

2 pounds shrimp	1½ teaspoons salt
4 cups water	12 peppercorns
1 rib celery with leaves	3 sprigs parsley
2 lemon slices	

1. Wash the shrimp and drain in a colander.

2. Place the water in a kettle. Chop the celery and leaves coarsely and add to the water. Add the lemon slices, salt, peppercorns, and parsley and bring the water to a rolling boil.

3. Empty the shrimp carefully into the water and simmer, uncovered, for 3 to 5 minutes. Small shrimp cook in

3 minutes, large shrimp in 5. Drain the shrimp and serve hot or cold. When hot shrimp are served, let each guest peel his own and serve with hot lemon butter or anchovy butter. Offer plenty of napkins and after the meal offer finger bowls or other small bowls filled with warm water and a lemon slice or rose petal. If cold shrimp are to be served, prepare the shrimp as indicated in the recipe for cold peeled shrimp and chill. Serve with a tomato cocktail sauce or a *rémoulade sauce* (recipe follows).

Yield: Four servings.

RÉMOULADE SAUCE

1 cup mayonnaise, freshly made if possible (*see page 81*)
1 hard-cooked egg
1 teaspoon anchovy paste (*see note below*)
2 teaspoons finely chopped sour pickles (*see note below*)
2 teaspoons finely chopped capers (*see note below*)

2 tablespoons finely chopped parsley
2 teaspoons finely chopped chives (optional)
1 teaspoon finely minced fresh tarragon or ½ teaspoon dried
Salt and freshly ground black pepper to taste
Lemon juice to taste

1. Place the mayonnaise in a mixing bowl.

2. Put the hard-cooked egg in a small sieve and using the fingers, press it through. Scrape off the sieved part that clings to the sieve into the mayonnaise.

3. Add the anchovy paste, pickles, capers, parsley, chives, and tarragon. If desired, add salt and pepper, a little at a time. Stir in a little lemon juice and mix. Serve with cold shellfish such as shrimp, lobster, or crab meat or with cold poached fish.

Yield: About 1½ cups sauce.

NOTE: Anchovy paste is available in tubes in many grocery stores and supermarkets. It will keep in the refrigerator for a long time.

Any sour pickles will do for the *rémoulade*, but the best, if they are available, are the imported French *cornichons*. These are available in many fine delicacy shops in metropolitan areas.

Capers are small, unopened flowerbuds plucked from caper bushes that grow mainly around the Mediterranean Sea. They are put up in brine in small bottles and are available in many grocery stores and supermarkets.

COLD PEELED SHRIMP

Let the shrimp cool in the liquid in which they cooked. Drain. Then, using a pair of kitchen shears, split the shrimp down the back shell. Peel off the shell.

With a small knife, peel or pare away the covering along the rim of the back of each shrimp. Pull this away and clean the small black or red intestinal tract along the rim of the back. If necessary, rinse the shrimp under cold water to remove. Drain the shrimp on absorbent toweling.

BUTTERS FOR SHRIMP

LEMON BUTTER FOR SHRIMP

½ pound (1 cup; 2 sticks) butter
1 tablespoon lemon juice or more to taste
Salt to taste, if necessary

1 teaspoon Worcestershire sauce
¼ teaspoon Tabasco sauce (optional)

1. Melt the butter in a small saucepan and stir with a wire whisk. While stirring, gradually add the lemon juice. 2. Taste the butter and see if it needs salt. The salt content of butter varies. Add the salt and Worcestershire sauce, stirring. Add the Tabasco sauce, if desired. Taste the sauce again. If more lemon would seem suitable, add it. Yield: About 1 cup (four servings).

ANCHOVY BUTTER FOR SHRIMP

Prepare the lemon butter for shrimp and stir in 1 tablespoon of anchovy paste. Anchovy paste is available in tubes. If it cannot be purchased that way, or if desired, simply drain 3 canned anchovy fillets and chop them.

BAKED LOBSTER À LA ANN SERANNE

The best recipe for baked lobster I've ever known is that of Ann Seranne, one of America's finest cooks and cookbook authors. The great wonder, as she has remarked before, is that restaurants throughout the country don't adopt this simple method. It is simplicity itself and provides the tenderest, tastiest lobster conceivable.

Please note that live lobsters must be used. If you are squeamish about killing a lobster, have it split by the fishman but the lobster should be used within the hour.

4 live lobsters, about 1½ pounds each	½ pound (1 cup; 2 sticks) butter
Salt and freshly ground black pepper to taste	Juice of 2 lemons

1. Preheat the oven to 350 degrees.

2. Place the lobsters, one at a time, shell-side up on a flat cutting surface. Plunge a heavy kitchen knife into the center of each lobster where tail and body meet. This will kill them instantly. Quickly bring the knife down through the body section and then through the tail section to cut lobster in half. Crack the claws with the knife. Remove and discard the tough sac near the eyes of the lobster but leave the green and red soft portions in the chest section. These are the liver (tomalley) and coral.

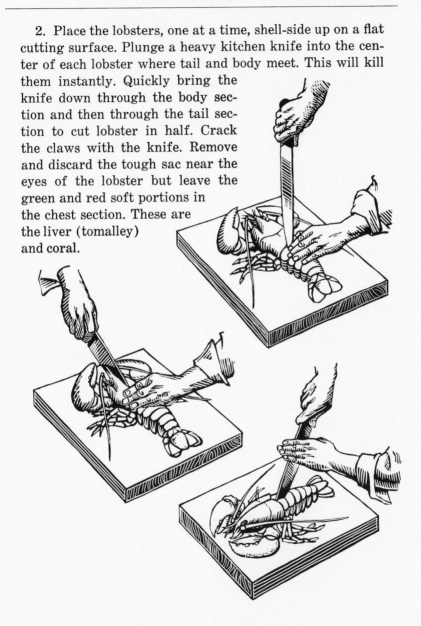

3. Arrange the lobster halves split-side up and side by side in a large baking dish.

4. Sprinkle the cut portions of the lobster lightly with salt but generously with freshly ground pepper. Arrange small pats (thin slices) of butter up and down the cut portions of the lobster. Sprinkle with lemon juice. Place the baking dish in the oven and bake for 15 minutes. Baste the lobsters with the juices in the pan. Bake for 15 minutes more. Serve immediately. If you wish you can serve the lobsters with lemon halves and with more melted butter, but it is not necessary.

Yield: Four servings.

POACHED FISH

To poach a whole fish (which means simmering gently in liquid until done) it is best to use a liquid—almost always water or water and wine—seasoned with vegetables and herbs. This liquid is called a court bouillon. After the court bouillon is prepared, it is best to let it cool before adding the fish. The fish is then added, brought to a boil, and simmered for 10 to 15 minutes for a whole, cleaned 3- to 5-pound fish. After the fish is cooked, it may be left in the liquid until it cools to lukewarm.

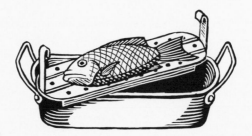

Leftover fish cooked in this manner may be mixed with mayonnaise for a salad.

1 whole, cleaned 3- to 5- pound fish, such as striped bass, sea bass, bluefish, large trout, or salmon	1 bay leaf
	2 sprigs fresh tarragon, if available
	1 sprig fresh rosemary, if available
Water	2 sprigs fresh thyme, if available, or 1 teaspoon dried thyme
1 rib celery	
2 carrots	
1 onion	Salt to taste
2 sprigs parsley	15 peppercorns

1. If available, use a long, oval fish boiler. If not, a roasting pan will do although it must be long enough to accommodate the fish. Many people prefer to cook and serve a whole fish with the head on. This is a question of choice, however.

2. Add enough water to the pan to cover the fish when it is added. Trim off and discard most of the leaves from the celery. Chop the celery rib and add it to the water.

3. Trim off and discard the end of each carrot. Scrape and slice the carrots. Add the slices to the water.

4. Peel the onion and cut it into slices. Add the onion slices, parsley, bay leaf, tarragon, rosemary, thyme, salt, and peppercorns. Bring the liquid to a boil and simmer for 20 minutes. Let stand until cool. If there is no rack to place the fish on, the fish may be wrapped in a cheesecloth "sling" to facilitate removing the fish from the court bouillon once the fish is cooked. To make such a sling, simply take a length of cheesecloth, wrap the fish in it and leave the ends long enough for lifting.

5. When the fish is ready to cook, place it in the cool

liquid and bring to a boil. Let the fish cook gently, that is to say simmer, in the court bouillon. Cook the fish for 10 to 15 minutes and turn off the heat of the stove. Let stand until lukewarm. Serve the lukewarm fish with melted butter, lemon wedges, and hollandaise or other fish sauce. When the fish is cold, it may be served with mayonnaise.

Yield: Eight to ten servings, depending on the size of the fish.

SOLE MEUNIÈRE

One of the most delicious ways to cook fish is in the French style called *meunière,* pronounced "mern-yehre." The word *meunière* means miller's wife and the dish is so called because the fish is dipped in flour before it is cooked. Almost any fish fillets or small whole fish can be cooked *meunière*-style, but the fish most commonly cooked that way are sole and trout.

This recipe is for *sole meunière.* To cook other fish in this manner, simply substitute other fillets or small whole, cleaned fish for the sole.

4 individual servings of lemon or gray sole fillets
½ cup milk
½ cup flour
1 teaspoon salt
Freshly ground black pepper to taste

4 tablespoons vegetable oil
8 tablespoons (½ cup; 1 stick) butter
1 lemon cut in half
Parsley for garnish

1. Place the sole fillets in a dish, such as a pie plate or baking dish, and add the milk. Let the fish stand in the milk for 30 minutes or longer. If longer, place the dish, covered, in the refrigerator.

2. Place a length of waxed paper on a kitchen table and spoon the flour onto the paper. Sprinkle with the salt and

pepper and toss or mix lightly to blend the seasonings and flour.

3. When ready to cook the fish, lift the fillets from the milk but do not dry at all. The fillets must remain quite wet from the milk. Immediately dip the fillets into the seasoned flour. The fish should be well coated on all sides.

4. Heat the oil and 4 tablespoons of the butter in a large skillet. When butter is hot, almost smoking, add the fish fillets. Reduce the heat to moderate. Cook the fish until golden-brown on one side, 3 minutes or longer depending on the size of the fish. Now, using a large spatula or pancake turner, gently turn the fish and cook until golden-brown on the other side, 3 minutes or longer. Cut four slices from the lemon and reserve for garnish. Squeeze the remaining lemon.

5. Carefully transfer the fish to a warm serving platter. Pour lemon juice over all and keep warm in the oven.

6. Quickly pour the oil from the skillet, taking care not to burn the hands. Wipe out the skillet with absorbent toweling and place the skillet back on the stove. Add the remaining 4 tablespoons of butter to the skillet. Let the butter cook until it starts to foam.

7. Pour the foaming butter over the fish and garnish the platter with the lemon slices and parsley sprigs. Serve with plain boiled, buttered potatoes.

Yield: Four servings.

About Broiled Fish

There is a vast variety of fish available to cooks in this country and a vast number of cuts that can be broiled. Thus, it is worth learning some generalities about broiling.

☞ In the first place, it is best to broil fish over or under very high heat.

☞ The fish, whether a whole fish or a fillet, should be cooked quickly, taking care that it does not overcook for it will become dry.

☞ If the fish is to be broiled in a home broiler, preheat the stove to its highest broiling temperature.

☞ Grease the pan that the fish is to be cooked on. Sprinkle the fish with salt and pepper. If a whole fish is to be broiled, sprinkle it both inside and out. Dot the fish heavily with butter or oil.

☞ If fish fillets with skin on are to be cooked, place them skin-side down. Place fish fillets (with or without skin) about two inches from the source of heat. It will not be necessary to turn them but they must be basted as they cook. Cook from 4 to 6 minutes or longer if necessary, depending on the thickness of the fish.

☞ Whole fish or very large fillets to be broiled should be placed about six inches from the broiler. Broil them for 6 minutes or longer to the side, turning once as they cook. The length of time will depend, naturally, on the thickness of the fillets or of the fish. Baste often. Serve hot with melted butter and lemon wedges.

SHRIMP ON SKEWERS

The word *kebab* has been accepted in the American lexicon as meaning "something on skewers." Thus people speak of "lamb kebabs" or "beef kebabs" or whatever kebabs, and in origin this is incorrect. *Kebab* is the Turkish word for meat. *Shish* is the Turkish word for skewer and, thus, more properly one should speak of lamb *shish,* beef *shish,* or whatever.

Every bit as good as meats on skewers are fish and shellfish. The important point about skewered things is that they be marinated briefly before broiling. The best of all marinades is a

French mixture made with oil and lemon juice, lime juice, or vinegar, plus whatever seasonings one desires.

Here is an excellent recipe for shrimp on skewers, and it illustrates the versatility of the marinade. If you have no taste for shrimp, use 1-inch cubes of swordfish or salmon.

1 clove garlic, finely
    chopped
⅓ cup finely chopped
    parsley
3 tablespoons lemon juice
    or lime juice
⅔ cup peanut oil or salad
    oil (do not use olive
    oil, the flavor is too
    pronounced)
Salt and freshly ground
    black pepper to taste
1 teaspoon chopped fresh

thyme (*see below*) or
    ½ teaspoon dried
    thyme
3 drops Tabasco sauce
    or to taste
32 medium-sized shrimp
1 large onion
1 large green pepper
12 cherry tomatoes
8 tablespoons (½ cup; 1
    stick) butter, melted
Juice of ½ lemon

1. Place the garlic in a large mixing bowl and add the parsley, lemon or lime juice, oil, salt, pepper, thyme, and Tabasco sauce. Beat lightly with a fork to blend. Add the shrimp and refrigerate for 1 to 2 hours. Stir occasionally to turn the shrimp in the marinade.

2. Meanwhile, build a charcoal fire or light the broiler and prepare the vegetables.

3. Remove the stems from the cherry tomatoes.

4. Peel the onion, then slice it into quarters. Pull the onion sections apart and cut the large outer sections into convenient rectangles to fit on skewers.

5. Split the green pepper in half. Trim away the core, pulpy white fibers and seeds. Cut the green pepper into rectangles the same size as those made from the onion.

6. Use four skewers. Arrange equal portions of shrimp, rectangles of onion and green pepper, and cherry tomatoes

in any desired manner. Place the skewers over hot coals and cook, basting with the marinade, until shrimp are done on one side. This should take about 3 to 5 minutes. Turn carefully and cook until shrimp are done on the other side, about 3 to 5 minutes. Baste once or twice as the shrimp cook. When ready to serve, push off one piece at a time onto plates or tomatoes will shatter. Pour hot melted butter seasoned with lemon juice over all and serve hot.

Yield: Four servings.

Meat and Poultry

How to Refrigerate Fresh (Raw) Meat and Poultry

WHEN RAW MEAT or fresh poultry is purchased and is to be used within a few hours, it may generally be left in the original wrapping from the butcher or poultryman. Or, if desired, it may be unwrapped, placed in a suitable dish and covered loosely with waxed paper. In any event, the meat or poultry should be stored in the coldest part of the refrigerator.

If the meat or poultry is sealed in clear plastic, the plastic wrapping should be removed. The meat or poultry should then be covered loosely with waxed paper and stored in the coldest part of the refrigerator.

Storage Limits for Fresh Meats

The storage time varies for various cuts and kinds of meat.

☞ Ground meat, be it hamburger, veal, or whatever, should not be stored in the refrigerator for more than one or two days.

☞ Stewing meats, such as cubes of beef, lamb, pork or whatever, should not be stored in the refrigerator for more than two or three days.

☞ With one exception, chops or steaks should not be kept in the refrigerator for more than three or four days. The exception is when the meat is placed in a marinade—generally made with wine and/or vinegar, oil, and seasonings.

☞ Large cuts of meat, such as large roasts, should not be held in the refrigerator for more than one week.

☞ Specialty cuts, such as liver, sweetbreads, and heart, should not be held in the refrigerator for more than one or two days.

How to Refrigerate Cooked Meat and Poultry

Cooked foods, such as roasts, should be covered or wrapped tightly before they are refrigerated. Clear plastic is good for this because it prevents air from getting to the food. If the food is not covered closely or wrapped tightly, air circulating around the food will cause it to dry out.

On Salting Meat Before Cooking

There seems to be a good deal of concern by many people as to whether or not meats should be salted before they are cooked. If there is a difference it is not really discernible at all, even to so-called professional palates. The vast majority of first-rate chefs in the world salt and pepper meat before cooking, and that is recommended in this book.

BEEF

There is no meat in the world as versatile as ground beef. It can be made into hamburgers and meat loaves and used in countless sauces. There are many people who prefer dishes made with hamburger to the finest sirloin or porterhouse. One of the reasons for the popularity of ground meat is the infinite ways to vary the flavor through the addition of herbs and spices.

There is one important thing to know about buying ground beef. It is best to have it freshly ground at the point of purchase or to buy it packaged from a source that is known to be reliable. Ground beef that is left to stand for a day or so, even in the refrigerator, develops an off flavor.

Also, do not look for bargains in ground beef. The product labeled hamburger is certainly no bargain. It contains a high fat content and, as the meat cooks, the fat melts and the meat shrinks. The meat should contain a little fat or it will be too dry. Buy good-quality beef, either ground round or ground chuck. Ground fillet or sirloin is an extravagance and they are generally too lean.

HOW TO MAKE THE BEST HAMBURGERS

The less the hamburgers are handled the better the texture will be. Thus it is best to add salt and pepper and other seasonings after the hamburger is cooked. When cooked, douse the hamburger liberally with butter and add such other seasonings including parsley, raw onion, fried onion, and so on as desired.

The following hamburgers, pan-broiled, are excellent.

1½ pounds ground round steak
Salt
Freshly ground black pepper

4 tablespoons (½ stick) butter
1 teaspoon Worcestershire sauce
¼ cup chopped parsley
Juice of ½ lemon

1. Divide the meat into four portions and shape each portion into a round patty. Handle the meat lightly, pressing

just enough so that it holds together. Sprinkle the bottom
of a heavy skillet with a very light layer of salt and heat
the skillet until very hot. Add the patties and sear well on
one side. Using a pancake turner, turn the patties quickly
and reduce the heat. Cook to the desired degree of doneness, 3 minutes or longer.

2. When the hamburgers are done, sprinkle them with
salt and pepper and top each patty with 1 tablespoon of
butter. Transfer the hamburgers to a hot serving platter
and sprinkle with Worcestershire sauce, parsley, and lemon
juice. Serve on buttered toast or on toasted buns.

Yield: Four servings.

On Pre-Seasoned Hamburgers

Although, as indicated above, the best hamburgers are those
that are handled lightly, you may be among those who prefer
a "firmer" hamburger. If you are, there are numerous interesting
seasonings that may be added and mixed into the hamburger.
You can, for example, make a "Rumanian hamburger" by mixing chopped garlic and salt to taste into the meat before grilling.
Or, a "chili hamburger" can be made by adding powdered chili
or powdered cumin and salt to taste.

CURRIED BEEF WITH PEAS

2 tablespoons butter
2 medium-sized onions,
    chopped, (about 1½
    cups)
1½ pounds ground beef,
    round or chuck or, if
    you feel splashy, top
    sirloin

1½ teaspoons salt
Freshly ground black
    pepper to taste
2 teaspoons curry pow-
    der
1 tablespoon ground
    coriander
¼ teaspoon crushed red

pepper flakes or more
to taste
1 cup (8 ounces) canned,
peeled Italian tomatoes
1½ cups garden-fresh

shelled green peas, if
available or 1 ten-ounce
package frozen green
peas

1. Melt the butter in a skillet and add the onions. Cook, stirring, until onions wilt. Add the meat, salt, pepper, curry powder, coriander, and pepper flakes. Break up the meat with the edge of a long-handled kitchen spoon. Cook for 10 minutes.

2. Add the tomatoes. Simmer, covered, for 20 minutes more.

3. Add the peas, cover again, and simmer until peas are tender, 5 to 10 minutes. Serve with rice.

Yield: Four to six servings.

CHILI BEEF WITH BEANS

2 tablespoons butter
2 medium-sized onions,
    chopped (about 1½
    cups)
1 or 2 cloves garlic, finely
    minced
1½ pounds ground beef
1½ teaspoons salt
Freshly ground black
    pepper to taste

1 tablespoon chili powder
    or more to taste
1 teaspoon cumin seeds
    (optional)
½ teaspoon sugar
1 cup (8 ounces) canned,
    peeled Italian tomatoes
1 cup (8 ounces) canned
    kidney beans, drained

1. Melt the butter in a skillet and add the onions and garlic. Cook, stirring, until onions wilt. Add the meat, salt, pepper, chili powder, and cumin seeds. Break up the meat with the edge of a long-handled kitchen spoon. Cook for 10 minutes.

2. Add the tomatoes. Simmer, covered, for 20 minutes more.

3. Add the beans, cover again, and simmer until beans are thoroughly hot—in about 5 minutes. Serve with a crisp green salad and French or Italian bread.

Yield: Four to six servings.

How to Make a Meat Loaf

If meat loaves do not qualify as food for the gods, then pity the poor gods. A well-made meat loaf, be it ever so humble in spirit, can be a delight for dining, aside from the virtue of economy. Here is an area, too, where the amateur cook can experiment almost without limitation, for variations on meat loaves are infinite and it is a pleasure to experiment with flavors and textures.

The important things to know about meat loaves are:

☞ Ground beef is the commonest meat used and yet combinations of pork and veal are excellent and in a sense more delicate. All or part of these meats may be substituted portion for portion for beef.

☞ Bread crumbs, within reason, give lightness and texture to meat loaves. Rice and other cereals may be substituted for bread crumbs.

☞ Almost any herb or spice used with discretion will add interest to a meat loaf. The commonest and best herb is parsley, but thyme, marjoram, and the like are good, too. Black pepper and chopped onion are fairly standard ingredients.

☞ Meat loaves are generally topped with slices of bacon or salt pork before baking to give flavor and to keep the meat loaf moist. Basting is not necessary.

☞ The usual time for baking a meat loaf is 1 to 1¼ hours to the pound of meat.

MEAT LOAF WITH CELERY

1 pound ground round steak
1 teaspoon salt
½ teaspoon freshly ground
　black pepper
2 slices bread made into
　crumbs (*see page 28*)
½ teaspoon chopped fresh
　or dried thyme

½ cup chopped parsley
1 egg, lightly beaten
2 tablespoons butter
¾ cup finely chopped onion
½ cup finely chopped celery
4 slices bacon
Tomato sauce (*see page
　95*)

1. Preheat the oven to 350 degrees.

2. Place the meat in a mixing bowl and add salt, pepper, bread crumbs, thyme, parsley, and the egg.

3. Meanwhile, melt the butter in a saucepan and add the onion and celery. Simmer gently, stirring occasionally, until onion is wilted. Cool slightly and add to the meat mixture. Mix all together with the hands. Shape the mixture into an oval loaf.

4. Rub an ovenproof pan or skillet with butter and place the meat loaf in the center. Cover with bacon slices and bake for 1 to 1¼ hours, pouring off fat as it accumulates in the pan. When the loaf is done, there should be no fat left in the pan. Let the loaf rest in a warm place for about 20 minutes, then slice and serve with any good tomato sauce (see page 95).

Yield: Four servings.

PARMESAN MEATBALLS

These meatballs, which are broiled, are simple to prepare and taste most unusual. They are an exceptionally good accompaniment for spaghetti with tomato sauce, and they are also delicious served as a luncheon or picnic dish.

1 pound twice-ground
   round steak
4 teaspoons Parmesan
   cheese
4 teaspoons bread crumbs
   (*see page 28*)

4 teaspoons butter, at
   room temperature
Salt and freshly ground
   black pepper to taste
4 lemon wedges

1. Place the ground steak in a mixing bowl and add the cheese, bread crumbs, butter, salt, and pepper. Mix the ingredients with the fingers until blended. Divide the mixture into four parts and shape each into rather fat meatballs. Do not flatten them like ordinary meatballs.

2. Preheat the broiler to full heat. Place the meatballs on a small rack in a baking dish. Place them under the broiler about four inches from the source of heat. Cook them for about 3 to 6 minutes on one side, then turn them and cook for 3 to 6 minutes on the other. The time will depend on how well done you want the meat. The meatballs may be cooked on a charcoal grill rather than under the broiler. Remove the meatballs and let them stay in a warm place for about 3 minutes. Serve immediately with one lemon wedge for each meatball.

Yield: Four servings.

On Cooking a Steak

There is no one on earth who could formulate a universal rule for the length of time it takes to cook a steak because of the many variables involved. The principal factors to consider are the thickness of the steak, the temperature of the meat when it is ready to cook, how close the meat is to the source of heat, and how hot the source of heat is. If the steak is cooked out-of-doors over charcoal, there is also the breeze to consider.

It is preferable that the meat be at room temperature before cooking. Therefore, an average-sized steak should be removed from the refrigerator about 1 hour before it is to be cooked.

The following rules of thumb, therefore, are only an approximation, but they will act as a guide:

☞ For a steak one inch thick, cook it for 3 to 4 minutes on each side if you want the steak rare. Cook it for 10 to 12 minutes to a side if you want it well done. The steak should be cooked four or five inches from the heat.

☞ For a steak nearly three inches thick, cook it from 10 to 15 minutes on each side for rare steak; 20 to 25 minutes to a side for well done.

☞ AND REMEMBER: nothing improves the flavor of steak like butter. After the steak is cooked, sprinkle with salt and freshly ground black pepper and put a generous amount of butter on top. Sprinkle with chopped parsley. Other additions for flavor are freshly squeezed lemon juice, a touch of Tabasco and Worcestershire sauce. A combination of butter plus the other flavors is not amiss.

On Roasting Beef

By far the most popular and elegant cut of beef for roasting is the standing rib roast. It is one of the easiest of all possible cuts to roast because it is more or less self-basting and no attention is required once the meat is in the oven.

Do not be put off by the variables to be found in standing rib roasts. It is necessary to outline and explain the most obvious, however. A 2-rib roast, for example, generally weighs from 8 to 10 pounds, untrimmed. It may weigh as much as 12. This is because the size of the ribs varies and so does the quality. A prime standing rib weighs more than a choice rib.

A 2-rib roast should serve about four to six people. The larger a standing rib roast is, however, the better, and for a buffet, for example, a 5-rib roast is just about ideal. Remember that cold leftover roast beef is delicious for sandwiches.

There are dozens of methods that are used for roasting beef and each method has its own advocate. Some recommend searing beef at a very high temperature before reducing the oven heat; others recommend cooking at a very high heat throughout the cooking period.

The following method is recommended because of its simplicity as well as for the excellent results that it produces. This method utilizes a constant, relatively low oven heat and once the meat is placed in the oven there is nothing more to be done until the roast is ready. WHEN THE ROAST IS COOKED, remove it from the oven and let the roast stand 20 minutes before carving. This will redistribute the juices inside the roast.

STANDING RIB ROAST

A 2- to 5-rib roast, oven   Salt and freshly ground
    ready   black pepper to taste

1. Remove the roast from the refrigerator at least 3 hours before it is to be cooked.
2. Preheat the oven to 325 degrees.
3. Rub the roast all over with salt and pepper. Be fairly generous in using both salt and pepper.
4. It is not necessary to use a roasting rack. Place the beef, rib-side down and fat-side up, in the center of the pan. Place the beef in the oven and leave it there, without

basting, until it is done. Use the following table to determine the correct roasting time.

Yield: Count on 1 pound of rib roast before roasting per person.

Consult the guide on pages 136–7.

On Boiling Beef

One of the most glorious dishes conceivable and also one of the easiest to make is boiled beef. Its preparation consists of nothing more than combining meat with vegetables and a liquid and letting the whole simmer on the stove until the meat is tender, from 2 to 4 hours.

Three of the best cuts of beef for the dish are flanken, brisket, and shin of beef. The shin, which has the bone, is the least expensive of all, and one large shin will serve an astonishingly large number of people. The best meat has a high fat and gelatin content. Very lean beef is not good for this dish because it will be tough and dry when cooked.

Leeks are not essential to the success of an eminently edible platter of boiled beef but they certainly do add something that no other vegetable can. When they are available, they should by all means be added to the kettle.

Boiled beef is not only delicious served hot from the kettle, it is also good cold. And the broth in which the meat cooks is excellent as a soup and may be used in other soups and sauces.

Leftover boiled beef can be used in making a famed French dish called *miroton* of beef, made with leftover onions, a touch of vinegar, and stock.

Recipes for boiled beef and sauces to accompany it follow. There is also a recipe for the *miroton*.

AN EASY GUIDE TO AN OVEN-READY STANDING RIB ROAST

Approximate Cooking Times—From:

2-rib roast	8 lbs.	Rare	2 hrs. 40 mins. to 2 hrs. 55 mins.
		Medium-rare	3 hrs. to 3 hrs. 25 mins.
		Medium	3 hrs. 30 mins. to 3 hrs. 55 mins.
		Well done	4 hrs. to 5 hrs.
	10 lbs.	Rare	3 hrs. 20 mins. to 3 hrs. 35 mins.
		Medium-rare	3 hrs. 40 mins. to 4 hrs. 15 mins.
		Medium	4 hrs. 20 mins. to 4 hrs. 55 mins.
		Well done	5 hrs. to 5 hrs. 55 mins.
	12 lbs.	Rare	4 hrs. to 4 hrs. 20 mins.
		Medium-rare	4 hrs. 25 mins. to 5 hrs. 10 mins.
		Medium	5 hrs. 15 mins. to 5 hrs. 55 mins.
		Well done	6 hrs. to 7 hrs. 10 mins.
3-rib roast	14 lbs.	Rare	4 hrs. 40 mins. to 5 hrs.
		Medium-rare	5 hrs. 10 mins. to 6 hrs.
		Medium	6 hrs. 10 mins. to 6 hrs. 50 mins.
		Well done	7 hrs. to 8 hrs. 15 mins.
	16 lbs.	Rare	5 hrs. 20 mins. to 5 hrs. 50 mins.
		Medium-rare	5 hrs. 50 mins. to 6 hrs. 50 mins.
		Medium	7 hrs. to 7 hrs. 50 mins.
		Well done	8 hrs. to 9 hrs. 30 mins.

4-rib roast	18 lbs.	Rare	6 hrs.	to	6 hrs. 30 mins.
		Medium-rare	6 hrs. 40 mins.	to	7 hrs. 40 mins.
		Medium	7 hrs. 50 mins.	to	8 hrs. 50 mins.
		Well done	9 hrs.	to	10 hrs. 50 mins.
	20 lbs.	Rare	6 hrs. 40 mins.	to	7 hrs. 10 mins.
		Medium-rare	7 hrs. 20 mins.	to	8 hrs. 30 mins.
		Medium	8 hrs. 40 mins.	to	9 hrs. 50 mins.
		Well done	10 hrs.	to	12 hrs.
5-rib roast	22 lbs.	Rare	7 hrs. 20 mins.	to	8 hrs.
		Medium-rare	8 hrs. 10 mins.	to	9 hrs. 20 mins.
		Medium	9 hrs. 30 mins.	to	10 hrs. 50 mins.
		Well done	11 hrs.	to	13 hrs.

IF A MEAT THERMOMETER IS USED TO DETERMINE COOKING TIME, INSERT THE THERMOMETER BEFORE THE MEAT GOES INTO THE OVEN. INSERT IT INTO THE THICKEST PART OF THE MEAT (see *illustration*). READING SHOULD BE AS FOLLOWS:

Rare	120 degrees
Medium-rare	130 degrees
Medium	140 degrees
Well done	150 degrees or more

BOILED BEEF

A 3- to 4-pound brisket of
 beef or flanken or a 4-
 to 5-pound shin of beef
Beef stock, fresh or canned,
 or water to cover (about
 2 quarts)
2 carrots, scraped and
 quartered
3 ribs celery, sliced

2 sprigs fresh thyme or ½
 teaspoon dried thyme
1 onion, peeled
3 sprigs parsley
1 bay leaf
1 leek, trimmed, split, and
 well rinsed to remove
 all sand and dirt
Salt to taste
12 peppercorns

1. Place the beef in a kettle or large saucepan. Add beef
stock or water to cover (about 2 quarts).
2. Add the remaining ingredients and bring to a boil.
Simmer for 2 to 4 hours or until the meat is fork tender.
Remove the meat, slice it and serve warm with warm vinai-
grette sauce (page 94), caper (page 80) or horseradish
sauce (page 80), and mustard.
Yield: Six or more servings.

MIROTON OF BEEF

4 tablespoons (¼ cup;
 ½ stick) butter
4 medium-sized onions,
 peeled and thin sliced
 (about 3 cups)
2 tablespoons flour
2 cups beef broth, fresh or
 canned

Salt and freshly ground
 black pepper to taste
1 teaspoon vinegar
1½ pounds boneless boiled
 beef, sliced (2 to 3 cups
 when sliced)
Bouillon potatoes (*see page
 186*)

1. Melt the butter in an ovenproof skillet or casserole
with lid. Add the onions and cook, stirring occasionally

with a two-pronged fork. As onions are stirred, the slices will separate into rings. Cook until onion rings are golden brown.

2. Sprinkle the onion with the flour and stir around briefly. Add the beef broth, stirring constantly. When the mixture bubbles up and is thickened, add salt and pepper. Onions naturally contain a good deal of sugar. To counterbalance this, add the vinegar. Partly cover with a lid and simmer for 15 minutes.

3. Add the beef slices and stir them around in the gravy until they are covered. Put the lid on and cook over low heat for about 30 minutes. Serve with bouillon potatoes (page 186).

Yield: Four servings.

LAMB

A Leg of Lamb

The easiest way on earth to cook a leg of lamb is to have it boned and "butterflied." That is, to prepare the boned leg so that it lies more or less flat on a grill or under a broiler. Thus prepared, it is as easy to cook as a chop or steak.

There follow two methods of cooking a leg of lamb. The first is for the "butterfly" technique; the other, for a whole, unboned leg.

BUTTERFLY LEG OF LAMB

A 6-pound leg of lamb
2 teaspoons salt
1 teaspoon freshly ground
    black pepper
2 cloves garlic, finely
    minced
3 sprigs fresh thyme or ½
    teaspoon dried thyme

½ teaspoon oregano
3 tablespoons red wine
    vinegar or lemon juice
½ cup dry red wine
½ cup olive oil
1 bay leaf
½ cup melted butter
Juice of 1 lemon

1. Cut away the thin skin from the top of the lamb, leaving the pure meat exposed. Bone the lamb as shown or have it done by the butcher.

2. Place the lamb in a large, flat container made of glass, enamel, or porcelain. Sprinkle with salt and pepper and rub the garlic into the meat. Sprinkle with the remaining ingredients and cover lightly with plastic wrap or

aluminum foil. Let stand in the refrigerator for 24 hours. Turn the meat occasionally in the marinade—that is to say, the liquid and seasonings.

3. When ready to cook, remove the meat from the marinade. Dry the meat with paper toweling and reserve the marinade. The meat may now be cooked under the broiler or over charcoal.

To broil:

Fifteen minutes before you are ready to cook the lamb under the broiler, set the heat control at its highest point. Before turning on the heat, however, remove the broiler rack.

When the broiler is thoroughly hot, place the meat, fat-side down, on the rack. Bring the liquid in which the lamb soaked to a boil on top of the stove. Slide the rack back under the broiler. The meat should be four or five inches below the heating element. Broil the meat for about 15 minutes or until well done and browned, then turn it, using a two-pronged fork. Spoon a little of the hot liquid over the lamb and continue broiling, this time from 10 to 15 minutes depending on how well cooked you want your lamb. Serve with the hot melted butter and the juice of 1 lemon.

To grill over charcoal:

Prepare a hot charcoal fire. The charcoal should cover an area slightly larger than the meat to be cooked. The coals should have burned long enough to develop a white ash before the meat is cooked. When the coals are ready, place the meat on the grill. The coals should be four or five inches beneath the meat. Immediately start basting the meat with the marinade. Cook meat for 6 minutes on one side, then turn and cook for 6 minutes on the other side. As the meat cooks, continue basting with the marinade. The meat should be well charred at this point.

Lower the fire bed or carefully shift the coals around. This will reduce the intensity of the heat. Continue cooking, turning once or twice. The total cooking time for medium-rare meat is 25 minutes. For well-done meat, cook for 25 minutes more. Serve with the hot melted butter blended with the juice of 1 lemon.

Yield: Eight servings.

ROAST LEG OF LAMB

A roast leg of lamb is also an incredibly easy dish to prepare. It is best to start the lamb at a high temperature, reduce the oven heat and continue cooking, basting only occasionally, at a low heat.

A 5- to 6-pound leg of lamb, preferably at room temperature	Flour for dredging Salt and freshly ground black pepper to taste
1 clove garlic, peeled	

1. Preheat the oven to 500 degrees.
2. Rub the lamb all over with the clove of garlic. Or, cut the garlic into very thin slivers and, using a small knife, make incisions here and there in the fat of the lamb. Insert the slivers. Sprinkle the lamb generously with salt and pepper and place lamb in a roasting pan. If a roasting thermometer is available, insert it into the meat at the thickest part. Make certain that the bulb of the thermometer does not touch the fat or bone of the lamb. Place the lamb in the oven.
3. Roast the lamb for 10 minutes, then reduce the oven temperature to 325 degrees. Using a large kitchen spoon, baste the lamb two or three times as it cooks. If you wish a rare leg of lamb, and many connoisseurs of good food prefer it that way, let it roast for about 1½ hours. If you wish it medium-rare, cook the leg for 1¾ hours. Or, if you wish it well done, cook the leg for 2 hours or longer. If a meat thermometer is used, it should register about 140 to 145 degrees for rare lamb; 150 to 165 degrees medium to well done; and 175 or more for extremely well done, which is the way many Americans prefer their roast lamb.

Serve the lamb with cooked dried beans such as pea beans, watercress salad, and a simple dessert.

Yield: Four to six servings.

FRENCH LAMB STEW (Navarin d'Agneau)

This recipe for a French lamb stew is a classic illustration of how any meat stew is made. First, the meat is browned in oil. The meat should be browned well in the oil but only a few pieces at a time. The reason for this is simple. The browning process seals in the juices of the meat. If, however, the cubes of meat are close together, they do not brown well and all the juices of the meat run out into the skillet.

After the meat is browned, seasoning and liquid are added and the meat is cooked until tender. Tomatoes, which add flavor, are considered part of the liquid because of their high water content.

After the meat is done or nearly so, other vegetables are added and cooked until just tender.

1½ tablespoons vegetable oil
1½ tablespoons butter
3 pounds lean lamb, cut into 2-inch cubes
1 cup chopped onion (about 1½ medium onions)
1 tablespoon sugar
3 tablespoons flour
Salt and freshly ground black pepper to taste
2 to 3 cups lamb broth or beef broth, fresh or canned

1-pound-1-ounce can peeled Italian tomatoes
2 cloves garlic, finely minced
¼ teaspoon thyme
1 small bay leaf
12 small red-skin potatoes, peeled
4 carrots, scraped and cut into 1-inch lengths
12 small white onions, peeled
1 cup shelled green peas or 1 package frozen green peas

1. Preheat the oven to 325 degrees.

2. Heat the oil and butter in a large skillet and add a few pieces of lamb at a time. The heat should be moderately high. Using a two-pronged fork, turn the meat around in the fat without letting the cubes touch each other. Keep cooking and turning occasionally until all the cubes are brown. As they brown, transfer them to a large casserole or Dutch oven. Add more cubes to the skillet and continue cooking. When they are all browned, add the chopped onion

to the skillet. Cook briefly just until onion wilts. Set the skillet aside.

3. Sprinkle the browned meat with the sugar and place the casserole over moderate heat for 4 or 5 minutes, stirring occasionally with a wooden spoon. Sprinkle the meat with flour, salt, and pepper and cook over low heat, stirring, for 3 minutes longer.

4. Add the broth to the skillet with the onions and bring to a boil, stirring with the wooden spoon to dissolve the brown particles on the bottom and sides of the skillet. Pour the broth mixture over the meat. Add the tomatoes, garlic, thyme, and bay leaf and bring to a boil on top of the stove.

5. Cover the casserole and bake for 1½ hours or until the meat is tender. Using a slotted spoon, transfer the meat to another baking dish. Strain the sauce into a 1-quart glass measuring cup. Skim off the fat that has risen to the top. Pour the remaining liquid over the meat and add the potatoes, carrots, and onions. Cover and bake for 25 minutes longer. Add the frozen green peas, cover again, and bake for 5 minutes more. Serve with rice.

Yield: Six servings.

VEAL

It is a pity that the quality of veal generally available in America is rather poor because veal is one of the most delicate and excellent of meats. There are, in fact, many French chefs who will judge a restaurant on the quality of the veal that is served.

The reason that first-rate veal is not generally available here is because of the expense involved. The veal, or calves, must be milk-fed and they require a tremendous amount of care. Thus it is more profitable for farmers to let the animals mature into beef.

The finest veal is best judged by its color. It should be a most delicate pink. Redness in veal is an indication of age.

Most Americans usually cook veal Italian style, and call it *scaloppine*. Actually *scaloppine,* or scallops, are very thin slices of veal, generally made from the leg. After cutting, the slices are usually pounded, which helps tenderize the meat. They must be cooked quickly. Breaded veal cutlets is one of the best recipes using veal scallops.

Breaded foods comprise some of the most delectable dishes in the world of cuisine. They are easy to prepare, and the breading requires three simple and rarely variable steps.

1. The pieces of meat, fish, poultry, or whatever are first coated lightly but thoroughly with flour.

2. The pieces are then dipped in beaten egg.

3. They are finally coated well with crumbs. The food is now ready to be sautéed in a little fat until golden on both sides.

BREADED VEAL CUTLETS

8 thinly sliced pieces of boneless veal
Flour for dredging
Salt and freshly ground black pepper to taste
2 eggs
2 teaspoons water

1½ cups fresh bread crumbs (*see page 28*)
8 tablespoons (½ cup; 1 stick) butter
8 lemon slices or tomato sauce (*see page 95*)

1. Have the butcher pound the veal slices until thin, or place them between sheets of waxed paper and pound them with a mallet or the flat bottom of a small heavy skillet. Remove the waxed paper.

2. Place the flour on a sheet of waxed paper and add salt and pepper. Toss lightly. Dip the pieces of veal, one at a time, in the flour. The pieces should be coated lightly but thoroughly.

3. Crack the eggs into a round glass pie plate, add the water, and beat lightly with a fork. Dip the veal in the egg to coat well on all sides.

4. Have the bread crumbs ready and place them on a large sheet of waxed paper. Dip the egg-coated veal in the crumbs to coat all over. As the veal is coated with crumbs, arrange the pieces on a sheet of waxed paper. Tap the pieces with the flat side of a knife to make the crumbs adhere.

5. Heat the butter in a large skillet or divide the butter into two skillets. When it is hot and bubbling, add the veal. Cook for 4 or 5 minutes until golden-brown on one side, then turn and cook for 4 or 5 minutes or until golden-brown on the other. Transfer to a warm platter and top each piece with a lemon slice or serve with a hot tomato sauce.

Yield: Four servings.

ROAST LEG OF VEAL

A 4-pound boneless veal
    roast, tied
4 tablespoons (½ stick)
    butter
Salt and freshly ground
    black pepper to taste

2 sprigs fresh thyme or
    ½ teaspoon dried thyme
1 whole bay leaf
1 whole clove garlic

1. Preheat the oven to 325 degrees.

2. Select a small pan for roasting the veal, one in which the meat will rest comfortably and with sides not too high. There should be room around the roast for scooping up the pan juices for basting the meat.

3. Place the pan on top of the stove and heat the butter. Add the veal and, using the fingers, turn the meat around in the butter until the meat is coated. Sprinkle with salt and pepper.

4. Sprinkle the thyme around the roast. Add the bay leaf and garlic to the pan. If a meat thermometer is available, use it. Stick the thermometer into the center of the roast and place the roast in the oven.

5. Use a heavy kitchen spoon to scoop up the fat and juices from around the meat to baste it. Baste often and continue cooking until the meat thermometer registers 160 to 165 degrees. You may cook the roast longer if you like it well done. Preferably, however, the roast should be slightly pink inside. The total cooking time should be from about 2 to 2¼ hours. Serve the roast, cut into thin slices, with the natural pan juices.

Yield: Six to eight servings.

BLANQUETTE OF VEAL

This is one of the most delicious veal dishes from the French kitchen. The recipe looks long but it is easy to make.

2½ pounds veal shoulder, cut into 1½-inch cubes	12 peppercorns or ½ teaspoon freshly ground black pepper
Water	
Salt to taste	1 bay leaf

2 sprigs fresh parsley
1 onion, peeled and studded
  with 2 cloves
2 carrots
24 small white onions
12 fresh mushrooms or
  ½ cup canned button
  mushrooms
6 tablespoons (¾ stick)
  butter

2 teaspoons lemon juice
Canned beef or chicken
  broth (optional)
4 tablespoons flour
Freshly ground black
  pepper to taste
2 egg yolks
½ cup heavy cream

1. Place the cubes of veal in a deep saucepan or kettle and add enough water to cover the meat. Bring gently to a boil and skim the surface as the foam rises. Cook, skimming as necessary, for about 5 minutes.

2. Add the salt, peppercorns, bay leaf, parsley, and the onion studded with cloves. Trim off and discard both ends of each carrot. Cut each carrot into quarters and add them to the saucepan. Cover the saucepan. Return the liquid to a boil and simmer until meat is tender, about 1½ hours. If the meat is not tender at the end of that time, continue cooking.

3. When the meat is done, use a slotted spoon and remove the meat to a warm mixing bowl. Cover with aluminum foil and keep warm. Return the cooking liquid in the saucepan to a boil and cook over high heat for about 5 minutes. This will concentrate the broth somewhat and strengthen its flavor.

4. Meanwhile, peel the 24 onions and place them in a saucepan. Add water to cover and salt and simmer, uncovered, until onions are tender but still firm. Do not overcook.

5. While the onions cook, wash the mushrooms (if you are using fresh ones) under cold running water. Drain, then trim off the stems even with the caps and discard.

Heat 2 tablespoons of the butter and add the mushroom caps. Sprinkle with 1 teaspoon of the lemon juice. (Rinsing the mushrooms and adding the lemon juice helps keep the mushrooms white.) Sprinkle the mushrooms lightly with salt. When the mushrooms are tender, remove them from the heat.

6. Strain the liquid in which the veal cooked. Measure the liquid. There should be about 2 cups. If not, add a little canned beef or chicken broth to make 2 cups. Bring the broth to a boil.

7. Using the fingers, blend the flour with the remaining butter. The mixture should be smooth. Add this, bit by bit, to the simmering broth while stirring constantly with a wire whisk or other beater. When the mixture is thickened and smooth, season it to taste with salt and pepper. Remove the sauce from the heat.

8. Beat the egg yolks with the cream until well blended. Add this to the sauce, stirring rapidly and constantly with a whisk. Return the sauce to the heat and cook, stirring, until mixture is thickened. Do not let the sauce boil or it may curdle. Add the remaining lemon juice and the meat. Add the onions and mushrooms. Heat thoroughly without boiling. Serve with rice.

Yield: Four servings.

PORK

Although a roast loin of pork is not a regal dish, it can be eminently delicious, particularly in the fall or winter. Cold left-over roast pork makes excellent sandwiches on bread spread with mayonnaise and coarsely grated black pepper.

The following is a delicious recipe for pork delicately seasoned with thyme. This roast is a good illustration of how herbs may be varied to advantage with a little imagination. For example, make this once with thyme and for the next occasion substitute a little chopped rosemary for the thyme. For those who like garlic, small slivers could be inserted between the fat and the lean of the roast before it is cooked.

ROAST LOIN OF PORK

A 6-pound loin of pork, oven-ready
1 tablespoon salt
1 teaspoon freshly ground black pepper
2 teaspoons chopped fresh thyme or 1 teaspoon dried thyme
½ teaspoon nutmeg, preferably freshly grated
2 carrots

1 large onion
1 clove garlic
2 whole cloves
1 rib celery with leaves
4 sprigs fresh parsley
1 bay leaf
1¼ cups dry white wine or water
1¼ cups fresh or canned beef stock
½ lemon

1. Preheat the oven to 450 degrees.

2. Wipe loin of pork all over with a damp cloth.

3. In a mixing bowl, combine the salt, pepper, thyme, and nutmeg and mix well with the fingers. Using the fingers, rub the mixture all over the surface of the pork but principally on the fat part. Place the roast fat-side up in a roasting pan.

4. Scrape the carrots and trim off both ends. Slice the carrots and scatter the slices around the roast.

5. Peel the onion and slice into thin rings. Scatter the rings around the roast.

6. Peel the garlic and, using the flat side of a knife,

crush it. Add the garlic to the other vegetables around the roast. Add the cloves.

7. Cut the celery rib into four or five sections and add along with the leaves. Add the parsley and bay leaf, then pour ½ cup of the wine or water around the roast. Add ½ cup of the beef stock.

8. Place the roast in the oven and bake for 20 minutes. By this time it should be golden-brown. If not, bake for 5 to 10 minutes more.

9. Reduce the oven heat to 350 degrees and continue roasting the pork. Use a large kitchen spoon and baste the roast with the liquid in the bottom of the pan. Cook the roast for 3 or 4 hours while basting. The longer the roast cooks the more tender it will become.

10. Using a two-pronged fork and the large spoon, transfer the roast to a serving dish and squeeze the lemon half over the roast.

11. Pour the liquid from the roasting pan into a 1-quart glass measuring cup. Using the large spoon, skim off the fat from the top. Pour the remaining liquid back into the roasting pan. Bring the liquid to a boil on top of the stove and add the remaining wine and beef stock. When the mixture simmers, use a wooden spoon to work around the bottom and sides of the roasting pan to scrape up the brown particles that cling to the bottom and sides. This gives flavor to the sauce.

12. Strain the sauce into a serving dish and serve the sauce with the roast pork.

Yield: Six to eight servings.

HOW TO COOK BACON

Place as many slices of bacon as desired in a large cold skillet. Heat the skillet and, as the bacon starts to cook, use a pair of tongs or a two-pronged fork to turn the slices. Continue cooking, turning occasionally, until bacon is as brown and crisp as desired. The heat under the skillet will affect the crispness of the bacon. If the bacon is cooked over very slow heat, it will not be as crisp as it will if cooked over medium-high heat. Take care not to burn the bacon, however.

When the bacon is sufficiently cooked, transfer it to a sheet of absorbent paper toweling or paper-toweling-covered cardboard stiffener to drain.

Remember that bacon fat may also be used in cooking. Many people like eggs cooked in bacon fat, and it may be used for making tomato sauces and other sauces that do not demand the subtlety of butter.

Poultry

ONE OF THE MOST INTERESTING DISHES in French cookery is also one of the easiest to prepare. Basically it is called a sauté of chicken.

There is a standard procedure for preparing this dish. The chicken pieces are sprinkled with salt and pepper. They are then cooked in butter until golden. They are transferred from the skillet and a liquid of some sort is added to the skillet. This liquid is scraped around to dissolve any brown particles that cling to the bottom and sides of the skillet and it is this that gives more color and flavor to the sauce. The chicken is returned to the skillet, covered, and cooked until the chicken is tender. That is all there is to it. By varying the flavors with different herbs and spices and by varying the liquids, the character of the dish may be altered at will.

CHICKEN SAUTÉ

A 2½- to 3-pound chicken, cut into serving pieces
Salt and freshly ground black pepper to taste
4 tablespoons (½ stick) butter
3 tablespoons vegetable or salad oil
3 tablespoons finely chopped shallot or green onion (scallion)
¼ cup dry white wine

1½ tablespoons flour
1½ cups fresh or canned
   chicken stock
½ bay leaf

2 tablespoons lemon
   juice
Chopped parsley
   (optional)

1. Place the chicken pieces on a flat board. Sprinkle one side with salt and pepper. Turn the pieces and sprinkle the other side with salt and pepper.

2. Place a large heavy skillet on the stove. The skillet should be large enough to hold the chicken pieces in one layer. Add 3 tablespoons each of the butter and the oil. Turn the heat to moderate, and when the oil and butter are quite hot but not brown, add the chicken pieces in one layer. Cook over moderate heat until the pieces are quite brown on one side—about 5 minutes. Use a pair of kitchen tongs and turn the pieces over to brown them on the other side—about 5 minutes. Turn the heat down to low. Use the tongs to remove the chicken pieces temporarily to a mixing bowl or other container.

3. Pour off most of the fat from the skillet but try not to pour out the brown cooking particles that mingle with the fat. Add the remaining tablespoon of butter to the skillet and when it melts add the shallots. Stir them briefly around with a wire whisk. Do not let the shallots burn. When they have cooked briefly, add the wine. Cook the wine until it has almost totally evaporated, but do not brown the shallots.

4. Sprinkle the flour over the skillet and stir with the whisk. Continue stirring while adding the chicken stock. When the mixture is thickened and smooth, add the bay leaf. Return the chicken to the skillet and cover closely. Simmer over very low heat for 10 minutes. Remove the cover and turn the chicken pieces. Cover again and simmer for 10 to 20 minutes more or until the chicken is fork-tender. Taste the sauce. Add salt and pepper if desired.

Stir in the lemon juice and, if desired, serve sprinkled with chopped parsley. The best accompaniments for this dish include buttered noodles or mashed potatoes.

Yield: Four servings.

The Endless Variations of Chicken Sauté. There are as many variations for a chicken sauté as there are particles of salt in the sea. The following is only a sample.

1. To the recipe as it stands you might add other herbs, such as chopped parsley or thyme.

2. You might add ½ cup or so of ham, cut into thin strips, about 5 minutes before the chicken is done. In that case you might add a leaf of sage along with the bay leaf.

3. To the recipe as it stands you might stir in ½ cup of heavy cream at the end and bring it to a boil. If you do this, you should add a little more salt and pepper to taste. And if you'd like to make that cream dish richer, you might beat an egg yolk into the cream before adding it (but be sure not to let the sauce boil or the egg will curdle). And, if desired, add ½ teaspoon or more crushed or chopped tarragon along with the chicken stock. Then serve the dish sprinkled with chopped fresh tarragon if available.

ROAST CHICKEN

The secret of a tender, juicy roast chicken is continuous basting, roasting in a hot oven, and turning the chicken. A chicken just stuck in the oven will make a tasteless dish.

A 3-pound chicken	4 small white onions
1 teaspoon salt	1 small clove garlic
½ teaspoon freshly ground	1 sprig parsley
black pepper	½ bay leaf

¼ teaspoon dried thyme (if fresh thyme is available, add 1 sprig in place of the dried thyme

4 tablespoons (½ stick) butter
½ cup water

1. In order to make this dish the cook needs, among other things, two well-padded pot holders, a large kitchen spoon, a heavy skillet with a handle, and a kitchen timer. The skillet should be large enough to hold the chicken with ample space around it to permit scooping up of the fat for basting.

2. Preheat the oven to 450 degrees.

3. Sprinkle the chicken inside and out with salt and pepper. Place 1 onion, the garlic, parsley, bay leaf, and thyme inside the chicken and tie the legs together securely.

4. Heat the butter in a large ovenproof iron skillet placed on top of the stove. Using tongs or the fingers, turn the chicken quickly in the butter. This is not to cook the chicken but rather to coat it with butter. Place the chicken on its side and scatter the remaining onions around it. Place the chicken in the oven. Start the kitchen timer. Set it to ring in fifteen minutes.

5. After about 5 minutes, start to baste the chicken with the butter in the skillet. Hold the skillet by the handle and tilt the skillet. While tilting, scoop up the butter with the long-handled spoon and spoon the butter over the chicken. Return the chicken to the oven. Baste the chicken again every 5 minutes or so. When the timer rings, turn the chicken to its other side. Set the timer for 15 minutes.

6. Continue basting the chicken every 5 minutes or so. When the timer rings, turn the chicken on its back. Set the timer for 15 minutes. Continue basting occasionally. When the timer rings, the chicken should be done. When the chicken is done, it should be golden-brown. Also, if the chicken is lifted up and the juices run out from the inside

of the chicken, they should be clear. If the chicken is not done, continue cooking for up to 15 minutes more. The total cooking time is from 45 minutes to 1 hour.

7. Remove the chicken to a serving dish and discard the string around the legs.

8. Use the pot holders to take the skillet by the handle. Place skillet on top of the stove and add the water. Bring this to a boil and cook for about 1 minute. Strain the sauce into a sauceboat. Serve the chicken and sauce with rice and a green vegetable.

Yield: Four servings.

BONED CHICKEN BREASTS WITH PARMESAN CHEESE

Although the technique of breading foods is standard in classic cookery, it is possible to vary the flavors involved. For example, herbs or spices may be added to the bread-crumb mixture and, as in this recipe, Parmesan cheese and nutmeg may be added. This is an Italian dish, and it points up an interesting idea about chicken breasts.

Boned chicken breasts are almost universally enjoyed in Italy. They are not only excellent to the taste, they are easy to prepare. Most butchers will bone and skin the breasts (remember one whole chicken breast when boned yields two portions). Or it is easy to do in the home with a small paring knife. Once skinned and boned, the meat should be pounded lightly between waxed paper. Pound with a mallet or the bottom of a heavy skillet.

2 large whole chicken breasts, each weighing ¾ pound	Salt and freshly ground black pepper to taste
½ cup flour	¼ teaspoon grated nutmeg
	2 eggs

1 cup fresh bread crumbs
  (*see page 28*)
¼ cup grated Parmesan
  cheese

8 teaspoons (⅓ cup)
  butter
4 lemon slices

1. Have the chicken breasts skinned and boned. Or do this at home. The skin may be pulled off quite easily with the fingers. Work around between the flesh and bone with a paring knife to separate the bone. From the two chicken breasts there will be four portions of meat.

2. Wet the fingers lightly and dampen each portion of breast. Place one portion at a time between sheets of waxed paper and flatten lightly using a mallet or the bottom of a metal skillet. Tap gently.

3. Spoon the flour onto a large sheet of waxed paper and season flour with salt, pepper, and nutmeg.

4. Break the eggs into a pie plate and beat lightly.

5. Pour the bread crumbs onto another sheet of waxed paper and add the cheese. Toss lightly to blend thoroughly.

6. Dip the chicken breasts lightly in the flour mixture. When coated, dip the pieces, one at a time, into the beaten egg, then in the crumb mixture. Tap lightly with the flat side of a kitchen knife to help the crumbs adhere.

7. Heat the butter in a large skillet and add the chicken pieces. Cook until golden-brown on one side, then turn. If necessary, add more butter to the skillet when turning chicken. Cook until golden-brown on the other side. The total cooking time is from 10 to 15 minutes. Transfer to a hot platter or individual plates. Top each serving with a lemon slice and serve.

Yield: Four servings.

ROAST DUCK

Perhaps the easiest of all roasts to prepare is the domestic duck of America. The reason is that the ducks are so fat that they do not require basting. The best way to cook a duck is to start it at a relatively high heat. You do not even need to put the duck on a rack in order to roast it. The only real burden is that the duck or ducks must be turned in the pan as they cook and the fat from the pan must be poured off as it accumulates. And one word of caution: be sure to use pot holder mitts or hot pads in getting the roasting pan in and out of the oven when pouring off the fat. Most ducks in most markets will be frozen when purchased. The best way to defrost them is to place them in the refrigerator overnight. This way the defrosting takes place gradually. Or they may be defrosted at room temperature for about 5 or 6 hours.

A 3- to 5-pound duck
Salt and freshly ground
   black pepper to taste
1 small onion, peeled
1 clove garlic, peeled

2 sprigs fresh parsley
   (*see note*)
¼ teaspoon dried thyme
1 bay leaf

1. Preheat the oven to 450 degrees.

2. Open the cavity of the duck and remove the neck, gizzard, liver, and heart. With the fingers, remove and discard the chunks of fat inside the duck if there are any. Sprinkle both the inside and the outside of the duck with salt and pepper. Put the onion, garlic, parsley, thyme, and bay leaf inside the duck. Lay the duck on its side in an open roasting pan—by "open" is meant a pan whose sides are only two or three inches deep with enough room for heat to circulate around the duck.

3. Scatter the neck, the gizzard, and the heart around the duck. You may add the liver or not as desired. Many people discard it. Carefully place the roasting pan in the oven and bake for 20 minutes if it is a 3-pound duck; 25 minutes if it is a 4-pound duck; 30 minutes if it is a 5-pound duck. Now, remove the roasting pan from the oven. Holding a large two-pronged fork inside the duck to keep it from falling out of the pan, pour the duck fat down the drain or into a receptacle. You may, of course, use a basting syringe but this takes longer and is more tedious. Now, using the fork, turn the duck onto its other side and place the pan back in the oven. Continue baking for the same length of time as you did for the first side. Once more pour off the fat and this time turn the duck on its back.

4. When a 3-pound duck has cooked for a total of *40 minutes,* or a 4-pound duck has cooked for *50 minutes,* or a 5-pound duck has cooked for *1 hour,* turn the oven down to 350 degrees. Continue roasting the duck, pouring off fat as it accumulates. THE TOTAL COOKING TIME for a 3-pound duck is about 1¼ hours; for a 4-pound duck is about 1½ hours; for a 5-pound duck about 2 hours. When cooked, the duck should be golden-brown and crisp. There are two ways to tell when the duck is done. Lift it up with the large fork and if the liquids inside the duck run clear (that is to say, they are not reddish), it is done. Or, prick the duck between the thigh and the leg. If the liquid runs clear, the duck is done.

5. Cut the duck in half or quarter it and serve hot. Leftover cold duck is also delicious served on a plate or in sandwiches.

Yield: Two or three servings.

NOTE: You may vary the flavor of roast duck by changing the herbs inside. For example, substitute a sprig of fresh or dried rosemary for the parsley. Or add fresh or dried ginger. You may give a very dark glaze to the duck if you baste it as it cooks with a mixture of soy sauce and honey.

ROAST TURKEY

THE STEPS IN ROASTING A TURKEY

1. If the turkey is frozen, it must be defrosted before cooking. Look at the chart that follows, which lists the time it takes to defrost a turkey. The time needed for defrosting can range from 4 hours to as long as 4 days.

2. The turkey is roasted in an open pan. It is covered before and during roasting with cheesecloth dipped in shortening.

3. If a pan gravy is desired, it should be made from turkey broth. The broth is generally made from giblets. Thus, it is wise to make the broth while the turkey is roasting (see page 168 for directions).

TO DEFROST A TURKEY IN THE REFRIGERATOR

WEIGHT OF TURKEY	DEFROSTING TIME
4 to 10 pounds	1 to 2 days
10 to 20 pounds	2 to 3 days
20 to 24 pounds	3 to 4 days

TO DEFROST A TURKEY UNDER COLD RUNNING WATER

WEIGHT OF TURKEY	DEFROSTING TIME
4 to 10 pounds	4 to 6 hours
10 to 20 pounds	6 to 8 hours
20 to 24 pounds	8 to 12 hours

Dressings for a Turkey

Almost everyone feels that a turkey isn't a holiday bird unless and until it is stuffed. Stuffings are infinitely variable and can be as elaborate or simple as anyone desires.

Generally speaking, ½ cup of dressing should be prepared for each pound of bird. For example, 2½ cups of dressing should suffice for a 5-pound capon but count on a little more just in case. Five cups of dressing should suffice for a 10-pound turkey, 10 cups for a 20-pound turkey, and so on.

The dressing expands on cooking and therefore should be put into the cavity of a bird loosely. Almost, but not quite, fill the cavity before trussing. Leftover dressing can be baked in a buttered skillet and served separately.

BREAD DRESSING

(Enough for a 10-pound turkey or other bird)

8 to 10 slices white bread
½ pound ground sausage
　　meat
4 tablespoons (¼ cup;
　　½ stick) butter
¾ cup chopped onion
　　(about 1 medium onion)
½ cup finely chopped celery
½ cup finely chopped green
　　pepper

¼ cup chopped parsley
1 teaspoon crumbled leaf
　　sage
Salt and freshly ground
　　black pepper to taste
½ to ¾ cup or can-
　　ned chicken or turkey
　　stock
2 eggs

1. Place the bread under the broiler or in a toaster and lightly toast on both sides. Cut the slices into small cubes and measure them. There should be about 4 cups. Pour the bread into a large mixing bowl.

2. Place the sausage meat in a skillet. Cook the meat thoroughly, stirring and chopping to break up any lumps. Do not brown. Pour off the fat from the skillet. Add the sausage to the bread cubes.

3. Melt the butter in the same skillet in which the sausage cooked. Add the onion, celery, and green pepper and cook, stirring with the spoon, until the onion is wilted. Add this to the bread-cube mixture. Add the parsley and sage and sprinkle with salt and pepper. Black pepper gives an excellent flavor to stuffings and perhaps it can be used with a little less discretion than usual.

4. Moisten the dressing with fresh or canned chicken or turkey stock. Stock can be made with the giblets, water, and salt, simmered until the giblets are tender. The cooked giblets can, in fact, be chopped and added to the dressing.

The amount of stock you add to the dressing is a question of personal preference. Some people like a "dry" dressing, others a "wet" dressing. The more stock you add, the wetter the dressing will become.

5. Break the eggs and beat them lightly with a fork. Add eggs to the dressing and stir to mix. Stuff the turkey cavity and stuff a little dressing beneath the flesh of the breast. Roast the turkey as indicated elsewhere.

Yield: About 5 cups.

NOTE ABOUT DRESSINGS. The character and flavor of dressings are easy to change. For example, herbs such as chopped thyme or tarragon may be added. Chopped hard-cooked eggs could be substituted for the sausage meat. Chopped mushrooms cooked in butter could also be substituted for the meat. A little cayenne pepper would give the dressing more piquancy, and melted butter could be added to make the dressing richer.

THE EASIEST WAY TO ROAST A TURKEY

1. Preheat the oven to 325 degrees.
2. Sprinkle the inside cavity of the turkey with salt and pepper. Stuff the turkey if desired.
3. Place the turkey breast-side up on a rack in an open roasting pan.
4. Using the fingers or a "mop" made of absorbent toweling, rub the outside of the turkey generously with shortening or butter.
5. Sprinkle the outside of the turkey with salt and pepper.
6. Dip a large length of cheesecloth in melted shortening or butter or rub the cheesecloth with shortening or

butter. Drape the cheesecloth over the breast of the turkey.

7. Place the turkey in the oven. Do not add water. Using a large kitchen spoon, baste the turkey once or twice with the drippings in the pan. Thirty minutes before the turkey is to be done, remove the cheesecloth. This will permit the turkey to brown. If it seems that the turkey is becoming too brown, cover it with a loose "tent" of aluminum foil.

HOW TO MAKE TURKEY BROTH FOR GRAVY

Turkey giblets, including
    the neck, heart, and
    gizzard
Water
Salt to taste

1 rib celery with leaves
1 carrot
1 onion
2 sprigs parsley
12 peppercorns

1. Place the turkey giblets in a large saucepan and add the water and salt. The water level should be about one inch above the giblets.

2. Trim off and discard the root end of the celery rib. Cut the celery into 1-inch lengths, including the leaves, and add to the giblets.

3. Scrape the carrot, cut it into ½-inch rounds and add.

4. Peel the onion and add along with the parsley and peppercorns.

5. Bring to a boil and simmer from 1 to 1½ hours. Strain.

Yield: 2½ cups to more than 1 quart, depending on the size of the turkey.

TIMETABLE FOR ROASTING TURKEYS

WEIGHT (unstuffed)	ROASTING TIME (unstuffed turkey)	ROASTING TIME (stuffed turkey)
6 lbs.	2 hrs.	2 hrs. 30 mins.
7 lbs.	2 hrs. 5 mins.	2 hrs. 40 mins.
8 lbs.	2 hrs. 10 mins.	2 hrs. 50 mins.
9 lbs.	2 hrs. 15 mins.	3 hrs.
10 lbs.	2 hrs. 30 mins.	3 hrs. 20 mins.
11 lbs.	2 hrs. 45 mins.	3 hrs. 40 mins.
12 lbs.	3 hrs.	4 hrs.
13 lbs.	3 hrs. 15 mins.	4 hrs. 20 mins.
14 lbs.	3 hrs. 30 mins.	4 hrs. 40 mins.
15 lbs.	3 hrs. 45 mins.	5 hrs.
16 lbs.	4 hrs.	5 hrs. 20 mins.
17 lbs.	4 hrs. 15 mins.	5 hrs. 40 mins.
18 lbs.	4 hrs. 30 mins.	6 hrs.
19 lbs.	4 hrs. 45 mins.	6 hrs. 20 mins.
20 lbs.	5 hrs.	6 hrs. 40 mins.
21 lbs.	5 hrs. 15 mins.	7 hrs.
22 lbs.	5 hrs. 30 mins.	7 hrs. 20 mins.
23 lbs.	5 hrs. 45 mins.	7 hrs. 40 mins.
24 lbs.	6 hrs.	8 hrs.

HOW TO MAKE PAN GRAVY
FOR ROAST TURKEY

1. When the turkey is cooked, remove it to a serving platter. Remove the rack from the roasting pan.

2. Pour off most of the fat from the roasting pan and add from 2½ cups to 1 quart of turkey broth to the roasting pan. The amount of broth will vary according to the size of the turkey. Bring the broth to a boil and, using a wooden spoon, scrape and stir the bottom and sides to loosen the brown particles. When they are loosened, strain and measure this liquid.

3. For each cup of liquid, use 1 tablespoon of butter and 1 tablespoon of flour to make the gravy. For example:

FOR TWO CUPS OF ROAST TURKEY GRAVY

2 tablespoons butter	Salt to taste, if necessary
2 tablespoons flour	Freshly ground ·black
2 cups turkey broth	pepper to taste

1. Melt the butter in a saucepan and, using a wire whisk, stir in the flour. When blended, add the broth, stirring vigorously with a whisk.

2. When the mixture is blended and smooth, season it to taste with salt and pepper.

How to Vary a Roast Turkey Gravy

Various things may be added to a roast turkey gravy. They include chopped cooked tender giblets, chopped hard-cooked egg, and chopped celery that has been simmered in broth until tender but still crisp.

How to Remove Fats from Sauces, Gravies, etc.

There are several ways to separate fats from sauces, gravies, etc. One way is to use a basting syringe. You may dip the syringe into the bottom liquid and squeeze the bulb to scoop the liquid up and into another vessel or you may dip the syringe into the fat itself and squeeze the bulb to extract the fat. A better way, perhaps, if there is time, is to refrigerate the liquid or fat in question. The fat will tend to solidify and it then may be easily lifted off or scooped off with a kitchen spoon.

VEGETABLES AND OTHER ACCOMPANIMENTS

SELECTION OF VEGETABLES AS TO COLOR, FLAVORS, AND
SEASON . . . THE PROPER COOKERY OF FAMILIAR
VEGETABLES, NEW IDEAS FOR OLD FAVORITES, INCLUDING
BRAISING, COMBINING, STUFFING . . . ON SALAD GREENS
AND THEIR PREPARATION . . . SPAGHETTI AND RICE
BOTH AS ACCOMPANIMENTS AND ONE-DISH ENTRÉES

Vegetables

If the American public seems a trifle apathetic, if not to say dyspeptic, about vegetables, it is probably not only because they were forced to eat them as children but also because the vegetables were so poorly prepared. In the nation's restaurants, too, vegetables are so frequently overcooked and waterlogged as to make them inedible.

This is regrettable because properly cooked vegetables can be a sheer delight.

In selecting a vegetable for a menu there are three things to be considered—flavor, color, and the season. If a fish of delicate flavor is to be served, the vegetable should not be robust. Asparagus, to choose one example, would be ideal. If the principal dish has a white sauce, the vegetables should offer contrast—tomatoes, for red, for example, and the green, perhaps, of string beans or garden peas. It is always best to serve vegetables in season, for obvious reasons.

ASPARAGUS

24 asparagus spears   Salt to taste
Water to cover

1. If the asparagus stalks are tough at the end, cut off the bottoms with a sharp knife. Cut off only one inch or so.
2. Place the asparagus spears, one spear at a time, on a

flat surface and, using a swivel-bladed paring knife, pare the spears lengthwise. Leave about two inches of the tips unpared.

3. When all of the spears have been pared, rinse the tips well under cold running water. Some asparagus is quite sandy. If this is noticed, soak the asparagus for 10 minutes in cold water, then rinse.

4. Place the asparagus in a large heavy skillet. Use an aluminum or enamel-coated cast-iron skillet. Add water to cover and salt to taste. Cover with the lid and simmer until the tips are tender. This should require about 5 to 12 minutes, depending on the size and age of the asparagus. Drain. Serve the hot asparagus with melted butter and a little lemon juice.

Yield: Four to six servings, depending on the size of the asparagus.

BUTTERED BEETS

The important thing about cooking beets is to leave both the root and a few inches of the stem end on before boiling. If the root is removed or the stem end cut away, the beets will "bleed" and lose color.

12 medium-sized beets	black pepper to taste
Water to cover	1 teaspoon or more sugar
Salt and freshly ground	3 tablespoons butter

1. Cut off the top from each beet but leave about two inches of each stem. Do not peel and do not trim off the root end. Rinse the beets in cold water and place them in a large saucepan. Add water to cover and bring to a boil. Simmer for 30 to 45 minutes—the cooking time will depend on the age and size of the beets.

2. Drain the beets. If they are to be served hot, they

may be cooled briefly under cold water, just to make them cool enough to handle. Using a paring knife and the fingers, pull or slip off the outside skin. It should slip off easily. Trim off the root and stem ends. Slice the beets back into the saucepan and add the salt, pepper, sugar, and butter. Cover. Return to the heat and toss the beets around to coat them with butter. Serve immediately. If the beets are to be served cold in a salad, refrigerate them without peeling or trimming.

Yield: Four servings.

CARROTS

There is no vegetable on the greengrocer's shelf that varies more throughout the year than carrots. And, they are available all year long. When new and freshly harvested in late spring or early summer, they are sweet, tender, and pencil-thin. Throughout the remaining seasons they range in length from 6 inches to nearly a foot, but they are nonetheless worthwhile.

NEW CARROTS

1 bunch carrots, fresh from the garden
Water or chicken stock to cover
Salt (optional)

2 tablespoons butter, melted
1 tablespoon freshly chopped parsley or dill (optional)

Tear off the tops from the stem ends of the carrots. With a paring knife, cut off both the root ends and the stem ends of the carrots. Use a swivel-bladed paring knife to scrape the carrots. Take care not to scrape more than necessary. Arrange the carrots in a saucepan and cover with water or chicken stock. If water is used, add salt to taste. Bring the carrots to a simmer. Partially cover the saucepan with a lid and cook carrots until tender, from 10 to 15 minutes, depending on size. Take caution not to overcook the carrots. They should be crisp-tender. Drain the carrots and pour the melted butter over them. Serve sprinkled, if desired, with a little chopped parsley or dill.

Yield: Two to four servings.

If the carrots you buy are large and look somewhat old, it may be best to prepare them in either of the two following ways, as carrots Vichy or whipped carrots. Both these recipes go well with roasts or fried dishes.

CARROTS VICHY

6 large carrots (about 1 pound)	2 teaspoons sugar
¼ teaspoon salt	⅓ cup water
2 tablespoons butter	1 tablespoon finely chopped parsley

1. Tear off the tops from the stem ends of the carrots. With a paring knife, cut off both the root ends and the stem ends of the carrots. Use a swivel-bladed paring knife to scrape the carrots all around.

2. Use a vegetable slicer or knife to slice the carrots into rounds about ¼ inch thick. Place the carrots in an aluminum or enamel-coated skillet and add the salt, butter, sugar, and water. Cover the top of the skillet with aluminum foil and place the skillet over medium heat. Carefully

shake the pan occasionally, taking care that the liquid does not spill out. Continue cooking until carrots are tender and all of the liquid has been absorbed. This should take from 10 to 20 minutes, depending on the heat, the age of the carrots, and the size of the slices. When the carrots are done, remove the aluminum foil and continue cooking briefly until the slices start to turn brown. Sprinkle with chopped parsley and serve.

Yield: Four servings.

WHIPPED CARROTS

8 medium-sized or 12 small carrots	2 tablespoons butter
Water to cover	Freshly ground black pepper
Salt to taste	Nutmeg to taste

1. Wash the carrots and trim off each end. Peel the carrots, using a swivel-bladed paring knife.

2. Cut the carrots in half or leave them whole and place in a large saucepan or casserole. Add water to cover. The water should be about one inch above the top of the carrots. Add salt and bring to a boil. Cook until tender but not mushy. Drain.

3. Put the carrots through a food mill or potato ricer and beat in the butter. Add salt, pepper, and nutmeg to taste.

Yield: Four servings.

CORN ON THE COB

The fresher corn on the cob is the better it will be when it is cooked. The corn should be kept refrigerated and should not be shucked until it is ready to be cooked.

Water to cover   8 ears fresh corn

1. Add enough water to a kettle to cover the ears of corn. Place kettle on the stove and bring the water to a boil. Do not add salt.

2. Meanwhile, place a long length of waxed paper in the sink. Shuck the corn onto the paper, pulling away and discarding as much of the corn silk as possible. Neatly break or cut off the ends of each ear. Fold the shucks into the paper and discard. Rinse the corn under cold running water.

3. When the water in the kettle has reached a full rolling boil, carefully drop the prepared corn into the kettle. Let the water return to a boil and when it does place the cover on the kettle. Immediately turn off the heat and let the corn stand in the water from 5 to 10 minutes. Serve immediately without further cooking. Drain the corn and serve it with butter, salt, and pepper on the side. The corn may stay in the water for as long as 20 minutes without damage to its flavor.

Yield: Four servings.

CREAMED MUSHROOMS

The domesticated mushroom at its finest has a snow-white cap and is free of blemishes, top to bottom. When chopped, mushrooms discolor quickly, but rinsing them in cold running water helps prevent discoloration. Mushroom caps are ideal for stuffing.

1 pound fresh mushrooms   Salt and freshly ground
4 tablespoons (½ stick)   black pepper to taste
   butter   2 tablespoons flour
1¼ cups heavy cream

1. Wash the mushrooms under cold running water and drain them. Pat the mushrooms dry with a clean towel or paper toweling. Slice the mushrooms thin.

2. Heat 1 tablespoon of the butter in a saucepan and add the mushrooms. Cover and simmer until the mushrooms are wilted and give up their juices. Add the cream, salt, and pepper.

3. With the fingers, blend the remaining butter with the flour. Add the butter-flour mixture, bit by bit, to the simmering mushrooms. Stir well after each addition. The butter-flour mixture will gradually thicken the mushrooms. When all the butter and flour are added, bring mixture to a boil and serve hot on toast.

Yield: Two to four servings.

COOKED SALAD GREENS

Cooked salad greens have always seemed a bit unusual to the average American and yet they are eminently delicious. Among the best of these are braised Boston lettuce and braised endive, and this is how they are done.

BRAISED BOSTON LETTUCE

6 heads Boston lettuce
⅛ pound salt pork or
   bacon
1 small onion, peeled, sliced,
   and broken into rings

1 carrot, scraped and thinly
   sliced
2 sprigs fresh thyme or
   ½ teaspoon dried thyme
1 rib celery without leaves

½ bay leaf
Salt and freshly ground
   black pepper to taste
¾ cup fresh or canned
   chicken broth

¾ cup brown sauce, or
   canned beef gravy
2 tablespoons butter

1. Preheat the oven to 350 degrees.

2. Place the lettuce in a large kettle of cold water and agitate the lettuce gently with the hands without bruising the leaves.

3. Drain the lettuce well and pull off one layer of large outer leaves. Trim off a thin slice from the stem end of each head but leave the core intact.

4. Return the lettuce to the kettle and add water to barely cover. Bring to a boil and cook gently for about 5 minutes. Place the kettle under cold running water and let the water run until all the lettuce is chilled. Remove the lettuce, one head at a time, and squeeze well to extract more of the moisture. Set aside.

5. Cut the salt pork or bacon into thin strips and scatter them over a 10-inch skillet with a cover. Scatter the onion rings, carrot slices, thyme, celery, and bay leaf over the skillet. Cook briefly until some of the fat is rendered from the salt pork or bacon. Do not brown. Arrange the lettuce over the bed of vegetables and sprinkle with salt and pepper.

6. Cook briefly and add the chicken broth and brown sauce. Bring to a boil and cover. Place the skillet in the oven and bake for 1½ hours. Remove the lettuce while hot and split each head in half. Arrange the halves symmetrically on a hot platter. Spoon the sauce through a sieve and pour the sauce over the lettuce. Top with butter.

Yield: Six servings.

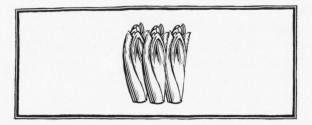

BRAISED ENDIVE

Like braised lettuce, braised endive is among the most elegant of vegetables. It goes best with beef, veal, pork, and lamb. Although this recipe takes time, it is easy to prepare.

18 Belgian endives	1 teaspoon sugar
⅓ cup water	6 tablespoons (¾ stick)
1 teaspoon salt	butter

1. Using a paring knife, cut off a small slice from the bottom of each endive. Place the endive in layers in a large saucepan or casserole and add the water, salt, sugar, and 2 tablespoons of the butter. Cover the saucepan or casserole with a tight lid and bring to a boil. Cook the endive for 30 to 45 minutes or until they are tender when pierced with a fork. Carefully pour the endive into a colander and let them drain well. Let them cool. This may be done several hours before the final cooking.

2. Heat the remaining butter in a large skillet and when butter is hot add the endive in one layer. Cook over medium heat until the endive are nicely browned on one side. The sugar used in the beginning to cook the endive should cause the vegetable to take on a brown-caramel look. Using a pair of kitchen tongs, carefully turn the endive in the skillet. Let them brown on the other side. Serve hot.

Yield: Six servings.

CREAMED ONIONS WITH TOASTED ALMONDS

18 small white onions
Salt to taste
⅓ cup whole, skinned,
    blanched almonds
3 tablespoons butter
3 tablespoons flour

¾ cup light cream
¾ cup milk
Freshly ground black
    pepper to taste
¼ teaspoon nutmeg
    (optional)

1. Preheat the oven to 350 degrees.

2. Do not peel the onions. Place the onions in a saucepan and add enough cold water to cover. The water should be about one half inch above the top of the onions. Add salt and bring the onions to a boil. Simmer until the onions are tender, about 20 minutes. Drain the onions and, when they are cool enough to handle, peel them with a small paring knife. Set the onions aside.

3. While the onions cook, place the almonds on a baking sheet or in a pie tin and bake until they are nicely browned, 5 to 10 minutes. Let cool.

4. Melt the butter in a saucepan and stir in the flour, using a wire whisk. When blended, add the cream and milk, stirring vigorously with the whisk. When the mixture comes to a boil it should be thickened and smooth. Cook, stirring, for 3 minutes or more.

5. Season the sauce to taste with salt and pepper. Add nutmeg, if desired.

6. Add the peeled onions and the almonds to the sauce. Bring to a boil and serve.

Yield: Six servings.

POTATOES

Almost any large potatoes sold in America are suitable for baking, whether they are labeled Long Island, Idaho, or California, and there are so many kinds it is hard to to describe them except in generalities. Generally speaking, the Long Island potato is of a fairly dark earth-color and has a relatively thick skin. Idaho potatoes are somewhat lighter in color and with a somewhat thinner skin. California "bakers" are the lightest of all and the skin is thinnest.

For boiling, the best potato is the relatively small, red, waxy-fleshed potatoes available mostly in spring and early summer.

BAKED POTATOES

4 large baking potatoes   4 tablespoons (½ stick)
Oil, lard, or bacon fat   butter
Salt and freshly ground
   black pepper to taste

1. Preheat the oven to 400 degrees.
2. With the fingers, rub the potatoes lightly with oil, lard, or bacon fat. Place the potatoes on a rack in the oven and bake for 1 hour or until potatoes are tender. To determine if the potatoes are tender, hold one of them between two pot holders and squeeze. The skins should "give" easily and the inside should feel soft.
3. Using pot holders, make an incision lengthwise from one end of the potato to the other. Press the sides with the fingers, using the pot holders to guard against heat. With a fork, loosen the inside of the flesh. Sprinkle the

inside with salt and pepper and add 1 tablespoon of butter to each potato. Serve immediately.
Yield: Four servings.

BAKED POTATOES WITH SOUR CREAM AND CHIVES

4 large Idaho potatoes,
  prepared according to
  the preceding recipe
½ cup sour cream

2 tablespoons finely
  chopped fresh chives
½ cup crumbled, crisp
  bacon

1. Prepare the hot potatoes exactly according to the preceding recipe. While they are still hot, arrange them on plates.
2. Pass the potatoes with the remaining ingredients and let all the guests serve themselves, spooning the sour cream into the potatoes and sprinkling, if desired, with chives and bacon.
Yield: Four servings.

BAKED POTATOES WITH CHEESE

4 large Idaho potatoes
Oil, lard, or bacon fat
Salt and freshly ground
  black pepper to taste
¼ cup hot heavy cream

4 tablespoons (½ stick)
  butter
1 to 2 cups loosely packed
  grated Cheddar cheese
  (about ¼ to ½ pound
  cheese)

1. Preheat the oven to 400 degrees.
2. With the fingers, rub the potatoes lightly with oil, lard, or bacon fat. Place the potatoes on a rack in the oven and bake for 1 hour or until potatoes are tender. To determine if the potatoes are tender, hold one of them between

two pot holders and squeeze. The skins should "give" easily and the inside should feel soft.

3. Cut each of the potatoes lengthwise in half. Scoop out the white flesh from each potato half. Press the scooped out portion, a little at a time, through a potato ricer into a mixing bowl. Add salt and pepper to taste. Beat in the hot cream and butter. Beat well until butter is melted. Spoon the mixture back into the potato "shells." Sprinkle each of the filled potato halves with ¼ to ½ cup grated cheese.

4. Line a baking dish with aluminum foil. Arrange the potatoes on the foil and return the potatoes to the oven. Bake until potatoes are thoroughly hot and the cheese is melted—at least 10 minutes.

Yield: Four to eight servings.

WHIPPED POTATOES

4 large potatoes (about
   1½ pounds)
Water to cover
Salt to taste
2 tablespoons butter, cut
   into cubes

½ cup hot milk
¼ cup hot cream
Freshly ground black
   pepper to taste

1. Wash the potatoes and peel them, using a swivel-bladed paring knife. Drop them as they are peeled into cold water.

2. Cut the peeled potatoes in quarters and place them in a large saucepan. Add water to cover. The water should be about one inch above the top of the potatoes. Add salt. Bring the potatoes to a boil and simmer until they are tender but not mushy. Put the hot potatoes through a food mill or potato ricer. While they are still hot, beat in the butter with a wooden spoon.

3. Beat in the hot milk and cream, a little at a time. Add salt and pepper to taste and serve hot.
Yield: Four servings.

BOUILLON POTATOES

This recipe for bouillon potatoes illustrates the flexibility of most recipes. The potatoes are cooked in beef stock or bouillon and this is what gives them their name. The potatoes can be, and frequently are, cooked in water with salt. They are good that way, too, but the stock gives the potatoes richness and body. The recipe below calls for new potatoes—those with the thin red skins—but large beige- or brown-colored potatoes may be substituted, provided they are peeled and cut into quarters.

12 new potatoes
Beef stock to cover
4 tablespoons (½ stick)
    butter, melted

3 tablespoons finely chopped
    parsley

1. Peel the potatoes and as they are peeled drop them into a saucepan and add cold water to cover. The water prevents them from discoloring as they are apt to do.
2. Drain the potatoes and add the beef stock. Bring to a boil and simmer, uncovered or partly covered, 15 to 20 minutes. The time will depend on the size of the potatoes. Test the potatoes with one prong of a two-pronged fork. They should be cooked just until tender in the center. If they are overcooked they will be mushy.
3. Drain the potatoes and add the butter immediately. Turn the potatoes into a hot serving dish and pour the butter over them. Sprinkle with chopped parsley and serve immediately.
Yield: Four to six servings.

SPINACH

The best spinach available are the tender young leaves from the garden. In metropolitan centers and during certain seasons, however, such spinach is rarely available. Spinach is one vegetable that travels well, however, and the thing to look for is dark green, unblemished leaves. Spinach is most often available in bulk or in clear plastic packages.

Spinach in bulk must be washed extremely well to remove all traces of sand. Spinach in clear plastic generally needs only one washing in cold water. When the spinach is washed it should be picked over to remove any tough stems.

Spinach should be cooked in as little water as possible, the water, in fact, that clings to the leaves when the spinach is washed.

1 pound spinach	¼ teaspoon nutmeg
Water	2 tablespoons butter
Salt to taste	

1. Wash the spinach well in cold running water. Pick over the leaves and break off and discard any tough stems. Drain the spinach and place it in a kettle or casserole. Do not add water and do not add salt. The salt has a tendency to make the spinach look dark. Cover.

2. Bring the spinach to a boil. It cooks quickly. When it has cooked for a minute or so, use a two-pronged fork to stir it around in the kettle, putting the cooked leaves on the top and the uncooked leaves on the bottom. Continue cooking, stirring the leaves occasionally, just until the leaves are wilted. That is enough. Drain the spinach and return it to the kettle. Or, if you desire, you may chop the spinach before returning it to the kettle. Season with salt and nutmeg and stir in the butter. Serve hot.

Yield: Two to four servings.

BAKED ACORN SQUASH

2 acorn squash
½ cup water
Salt to taste

4 tablespoons (½ stick) butter
4 teaspoons brown sugar
Nutmeg to taste

1. Preheat the oven to 375 degrees.
2. Cut each squash in half and scoop out the fibers and seeds.
3. Place the squash halves, cut-side down, in a baking dish. Pour the water around the squash and cover the dish closely with aluminum foil. Bake for about 40 minutes or until squash is tender. To test for doneness, insert a fork or knife inside the squash flesh.
4. When tender, turn the squash cut-side up. Sprinkle with salt. Add equal portions of butter, brown sugar, and nutmeg to the center of each squash half and bake uncovered until the sugar melts.

Yield: Four servings.

TOMATOES

In all of vegetabledom, there is nothing to equal the tomato. In late summer this large, red, ripe, vainglorious fruit is a prize simply eaten out of hand while warm. The tomato is equally prized in Neapolitan cookery, which tends to be robust, and in French cuisine, at its best the world's subtlest. There follow two easily prepared tomato appetizers, one French, made simply with sliced tomatoes with herbs; the other Italian, consisting of broiled tomato halves served cold.

TOMATOES VINAIGRETTE

2 large, red, ripe tomatoes
Salt
Freshly ground black
pepper to taste
½ cup finely chopped
onion

¼ cup finely chopped
parsley
3 tablespoons wine vinegar
½ cup olive oil

1. For this recipe it is not necessary to peel the tomatoes. Wash them under cold running water and dry with paper toweling. Cut off a thin slice at the base. Pare into and around the stem and discard the core. Slice the tomatoes onto a round serving dish, arranging the slices neatly. Sprinkle the slices with salt. The important thing to know is that raw tomatoes, more than any other vegetable, take well to a more than customary amount of salt. They also take well, oddly enough, to a large amount of vinegar.

2. When the tomatoes are sprinkled with salt, add the pepper. Scatter the onions over the slices, then sprinkle with the parsley, vinegar, and oil. This dish is especially good with a crusty loaf of French bread.

Yield: Four servings.

NEAPOLITAN TOMATO HALVES

This cold appetizer, served as a first course, is admirably suited to an antipasto that might also include cold tuna with

lemon wedges, pimientos, flat anchovies, black olives, hot Italian
green peppers, sliced salami, and the like.

4 firm-fleshed but ripe
  tomatoes
1 or 2 cloves garlic
Oil
Salt and freshly ground
  black pepper to taste
	1 teaspoon chopped fresh
	  rosemary or ½ teaspoon
	  dried rosemary
	1 tablespoon chopped fresh
	  basil

1. The tomatoes for this recipe should not be peeled.
Pare into and around the stem end and discard the core.
Slice each tomato in half.

2. Cut the garlic lengthwise into very thin slivers. Make
several small gashes into the cut portions of the tomatoes
and stash each gash with a sliver of garlic.

3. Oil a baking dish and arrange the tomatoes on it.
Sprinkle the tomatoes with salt and pepper. Liberally
sprinkle the tomatoes with oil, then sprinkle with rosemary. Place them under a medium broiler flame and let
them cook gently until hot and bubbling and the edges of
the tomatoes start to burn. Remove the baking dish and let
it stand until the tomatoes are cold. Sprinkle the tomatoes
with basil and serve cold.

Yield: Four servings.

STUFFED VEGETABLES

There are many good things about stuffed vegetables, among
them, taste and economy. Stuffed vegetables are also interesting
to prepare and are a welcome change from grilled steaks and

chops; as an entrée smaller casings, such as mushrooms provide, filled with a tasty stuffing make delicious hors d'oeuvres. Among the vegetables that take naturally to stuffing are green peppers. The peppers should have a bright or dark green skin. They should be glossy, firm, and free of blemishes.

PEPPERS STUFFED WITH PORK AND HERBS

6 firm green peppers
Boiling water to cover
4 tablespoons (½ stick) butter
½ cup finely chopped onion
1 clove garlic, finely minced
1½ pounds lean ground pork
½ pound mushrooms, chopped

1½ cups fresh bread crumbs (*see page 28*)
Salt and freshly ground black pepper to taste
2 tablespoons finely chopped parsley
½ teaspoon finely chopped rosemary
¼ cup grated Parmesan cheese
¾ cup water or tomato sauce

1. Preheat the oven to 350 degrees.

2. Cut a slice off the stem ends of the peppers and discard it. Using the fingers and a paring knife, carefully pare away the white pith inside the peppers. Shake out the seeds.

3. Have a kettle ready with enough boiling water in it to cover the peppers. Drop in the peppers and let them cook for 5 minutes. Drain them immediately in a colander.

4. In a large skillet, melt the butter and cook the onion and garlic until onion is wilted. Add the pork and cook, breaking up the meat with a slotted spoon. Cook until the pork loses color. Add the mushrooms and cook, stirring,

for 3 minutes more. Add the bread crumbs, salt, pepper, parsley, and rosemary. Spoon equal amounts of the mixture into the pepper cases. Sprinkle equal amounts of cheese onto the stuffing and arrange the peppers in a baking dish.

Pour the water or tomato sauce around them and bake until peppers are tender, about 25 minutes.

Yield: Six servings.

MUSHROOMS STUFFED WITH TUNA

12 large or 24 medium-
   sized mushrooms
6 tablespoons (¾ stick)
   butter
½ cup finely chopped onion
   (about 1 small onion)
1 7-ounce can tuna
1 teaspoon lemon juice
Cayenne pepper or Tabasco
   sauce to taste
1 cup cooked rice (see
   page 208)

Salt and freshly ground
   black pepper to taste
2 tablespoons chopped fresh
   dill or parsley or a mixture of both
1 teaspoon chopped fresh
   thyme or ½ teaspoon
   dried thyme
¼ cup buttered bread
   crumbs (see page 28)

1. Preheat the oven to 375 degrees.
2. Rinse the mushrooms in cold running water and pat

them dry with paper toweling. Remove the mushroom stems and chop them finely.

3. Melt 2 tablespoons of the butter in a small skillet and cook the onion until wilted. Add the chopped mushroom stems and cook until soft, stirring occasionally.

4. Open the can of tuna and do not drain it. Empty the contents of the can into a mixing bowl. Add the onion-and–mushroom-stem mixture, then the lemon juice, cayenne pepper or Tabasco, rice, salt, pepper, dill, and thyme.

5. Melt the remaining butter and dip the mushroom caps in it. Arrange them in a buttered, shallow baking dish and fill the caps with the tuna mixture. Sprinkle with bread crumbs. Bake for 15 minutes or until thoroughly hot and browned. Serve as an appetizer or as a luncheon dish with salad.

Yield: Six to eight servings.

TOMATOES WITH CURRIED CHICKEN

Like green peppers, tomatoes provide a natural case for stuffed foods. Tomatoes for stuffing should be firm, deep red, ripe, and free from blemishes.

6 large, red, ripe tomatoes
Salt
4 tablespoons (½ stick) butter
1 cup finely chopped onion (about 1½ medium onions)
2 cloves garlic, finely minced
½ cup chopped celery
2 tablespoons curry powder or to taste

2 tablespoons flour
1½ cups fresh or canned chicken broth
2 cups diced cooked chicken
1 cup cooked rice (*see page 208*)
Freshly ground black pepper
⅓ cup buttered bread crumbs (*see page 28*)

1. Cut a slice from the stem end of the tomatoes and discard it. Using a spoon or knife, carefully work out the pulp from the tomatoes and reserve. Do not puncture the shell of the tomatoes.

2. Sprinkle the inside of the tomatoes generously with salt. Let stand for 5 minutes, then turn upside down on a rack to drain.

3. Preheat the oven to 375 degrees.

4. Melt the butter and cook the onion, garlic, and celery until onion is tender. Add the curry powder and cook, stirring, for 2 minutes more. Sprinkle with the flour, then gradually stir in the chicken broth. Cook until mixture is thickened. Add the chicken and rice and season to taste with salt and pepper. Let cool slightly.

5. Spoon the mixture into the tomato cases and sprinkle with equal amounts of crumbs. Arrange the stuffed tomatoes on an oiled baking dish and bake for 15 to 20 minutes until tomatoes are piping hot and cooked.

Yield: Six servings.

EGGPLANT WITH BEEF

Eggplants are the king (or is it the queen?) of stuffed vegetables. There are a dozen or more techniques for preparing the shells for filling, but this is one of the easiest. The stuffing for this dish may be varied endlessly with the addition of various herbs. Almost all of the sweet herbs, such as parsley, tarragon, and basil, go well with eggplant and so do a multitude of spices, such as oregano and nutmeg. The following is eggplant as a main dish for lunch or dinner.

3 medium-sized eggplants
Boiling water to cover
2 tablespoons butter or
    vegetable oil
1 onion, chopped (about
    ¾ cup)
2 cloves garlic, finely
    minced
½ cup finely chopped green
    pepper
½ cup finely chopped celery
1 pound ground round steak

Salt and freshly ground
    black pepper to taste
2 tablespoons finely
    chopped parsley
½ cup grated Parmesan
    cheese
¼ cup bread crumbs (*see
    page 28*)
2 tablespoons tomato
    purée or tomato paste
12 strips bacon

1. The eggplants should be dark-skinned and shiny. When pressed with the fingers, the feel should be firm.

2. Bring a large kettle of water to a boil on top of the stove and drop in the eggplants. Cover and simmer for 15 minutes. Drain the eggplants and, when they are manageable, cut them in half lengthwise. Using a spoon, carefully scoop out and reserve the pulp, leaving a shell ½ inch thick.

3. Preheat the oven to 350 degrees.

4. Heat the butter and add the onion, garlic, green pepper, and celery. Cook, stirring, until onion is wilted. Add the meat and cook, breaking up any lumps with a slotted spoon. Cook until meat loses its red color. Chop the eggplant pulp and add it to the meat. Add the salt, pepper, parsley, cheese, bread crumbs, and tomato purée.

5. Fill the prepared shells with the mixture and top each filled shell with 2 strips of bacon. Arrange the shells on a greased baking dish and bake for 45 minutes to 1

hour. Serve hot as a main course with tomato sauce (see page 95).

Yield: Six or more servings.

SHRIMP-STUFFED EGGPLANT

2 large eggplants
6 tablespoons (¾ stick) butter
1 onion, finely chopped
1 clove garlic, finely minced
1 green pepper, cored, seeded, and finely chopped
2 ribs celery, finely chopped
½ cup finely chopped parsley
1 teaspoon chopped fresh
thyme or ½ teaspoon dried thyme
1 cup cooked shrimp, coarsely chopped
Salt and freshly ground black pepper to taste
1 teaspoon Worcestershire sauce
⅛ teaspoon cayenne pepper
2 eggs
4 slices very dry toast
¼ cup Parmesan cheese

1. Preheat the oven to 350 degrees.

2. Split the eggplants in half and scoop out the flesh from each center, leaving a shell about ¼ inch thick for refilling. Drop the eggplant flesh into boiling salted water and cook until tender, about 5 minutes. Drain the eggplant in a colander. Cover the eggplant shells with boiling water and let stand for 5 minutes. Drain.

3. Melt half the butter and cook the onion, garlic, green pepper, and celery until onion is translucent. Add the eggplant flesh, parsley, thyme, shrimp, salt, pepper, Worcestershire sauce, and cayenne.

4. Add the eggs to the eggplant mixture. Cook, stirring, for about 5 minutes. Fill the eggplant shells with the mixture.

5. Make crumbs with the toast, using a grater or an

electric blender, and sprinkle them over the filled egg-plants. Melt the remaining butter and pour over the egg-plants. Bake for 20 to 30 minutes. Sprinkle with Parmesan cheese. Serve hot.

Yield: Four to six servings.

AVOCADOS

When avocados are selected for a salad, the skin should be firm but with light pressure you should be able to determine that the inside flesh is soft. (This is reminiscent of the sign in one greengrocer's window: "If you must pinch the fruit, please pinch the coconut.") The avocado skin should be uniformly green and unblemished. The blemish indicates a bruise and it also indicates that the inside flesh will be dark.

Avocados, once they are cut in half, darken quickly and it is best to rub the cut surface with lemon immediately. Or, if the slices are to be tossed in a salad, the lemon juice should be added immediately. The lemon will prevent the avocado from darkening.

To serve avocado halves, run a stainless-steel knife all around the fruit lengthwise. Remove and discard the pit. Rub the cut surface with lemon and serve stuffed, if desired, with seafood and mayonnaise or with a simple, well-seasoned French dressing.

BEET-AND-GREENS SALAD

Beets are delicious served cold in a salad. They should be peeled and trimmed and sliced into a salad bowl. They may then be served with a simple French dressing. For 12 sliced beets, toss them with 1 tablespoon wine vinegar, 3 tablespoons olive oil, and salt and freshly ground black pepper to taste.

Beets for salad are also delicious when combined with other vegetables, particularly celery and Belgian endive. Simply make the salad as indicated above and add about 1 cup chopped celery hearts or 2 sliced, trimmed Belgian endives.

PICKLED BEETS

6 medium-sized beets
Water to cover
Salt to taste
10 peppercorns
2 teaspoons pickling spices

1 tablespoon sugar
Freshly ground black
  pepper to taste
½ cup red wine vinegar

1. Do not peel the beets. Do not trim off the stem end. Cut off the beet greens about two inches from the top of the beets. The reason for this is as follows: if the beets are cut, the color will drain from them as they cook.

2. Place the beets in a large saucepan and add water to cover. The water should cover the top of the beets by about one inch. Add the salt and peppercorns and bring to a boil. Simmer, partly covered, until the beets are tender. The cooking time will vary from about 45 minutes to 2 hours, depending on the age and size of the beets. To test the beets, it is necessary to penetrate them with a two-pronged fork or other sharp instrument. If the tines go in easily, the beets are done.

3. Drain the beets and run them under cold running water until they are cool enough to handle. Peel the beets (the skin slips off easily) and trim off both ends. Slice the beets into a mixing bowl. Sprinkle with the spices, sugar,

pepper, and vinegar. Refrigerate until ready to serve.
Yield: Four servings.

CUCUMBERS

Cucumbers, particularly if they are fresh from the garden (although store-bought ones are very good), are one of the most excellent vegetables. Properly made, they are crisp and there are few vegetables likelier to refresh the palate. Here are two summery ways to prepare cucumbers, one with sour cream, the other in the Swedish manner.

CUCUMBERS WITH SOUR CREAM

2 large or 4 small
  cucumbers
Salt to taste
1½ tablespoons wine
  vinegar
1½ cups sour cream
½ teaspoon sugar

Freshly ground black
  pepper to taste
3 tablespoons finely
  chopped scallions
  (green onions), chives,
  or dill

1. Using a swivel-bladed paring knife, pare away the peel of the cucumbers. Using a knife or a vegetable slicer, cut the cucumbers into thin slices (about ⅛ inch thick).

2. Sprinkle the cucumbers with salt and vinegar and toss briefly.

3. Combine the remaining ingredients in a mixing bowl and, when blended, stir in the cucumbers. Toss well and serve.

Yield: Four servings.

SWEDISH CUCUMBERS

2 large or 4 small cucumbers	1 teaspoon sugar
	1 ice cube
Salt and freshly ground black pepper to taste	1 tablespoon freshly chopped dill or 1 teaspoon dried dill
2 tablespoons wine vinegar	

1. Using a swivel-bladed paring knife, pare away the peel of the cucumbers. Using a knife or a vegetable slicer, cut the cucumbers into thin slices (about ⅛ inch thick).

2. Sprinkle the cucumbers with salt and pepper. Add the remaining ingredients and toss. Serve cold.

Yield: Four servings.

COTTAGE CHEESE WITH CUCUMBER

Cottage cheese as an ingredient, like potatoes and noodles, borrows character from whatever it is combined with. It takes well to cucumbers, scallions, and mayonnaise, and a combination of the four is a joy for a light snack or as a side dish for hamburgers and other broiled dishes.

1 cucumber	Juice of ½ lemon
3 scallions (green onions)	Salt and freshly ground black pepper to taste
1 pint (2 cups) cottage cheese (preferably large curd)	Few drops Tabasco sauce
	Tomato slices or lettuce leaves or both
4 to 6 tablespoons mayonnaise	

1. Use a swivel-bladed paring knife and peel the cucumber lengthwise. Trim off the ends. Split the cucumber in half and, using a small spoon, scoop out the seeds.

2. Place half the cucumber on a flat chopping board. Using a sharp knife, slice the cucumber lengthwise at ¼-inch intervals. Hold the lengths of cucumber in one hand and chop cucumber crosswise to make small pieces.

3. Trim off the root end of the scallions. Cut off about 5 inches from the tops of the scallions. Pull off and discard the outer leaves of the scallions. Using a sharp knife, cut the scallions crosswise into small rings.

4. Spoon the cottage cheese into a mixing bowl.

5. Add the cucumbers, scallions, and mayonnaise. Using a fork, stir the mixture to blend. Add lemon juice and salt and pepper to taste. Add the Tabasco and stir. Serve the salad on slices of tomato or on lettuce leaves or both.

Yield: Four to six servings.

On Salad Bowls

Whoever thought up the idea that salad bowls should not be washed should be tossed summarily into a pot of rancid oil. Unwashed salad bowls quickly become stale no matter how they are otherwise cleaned. If a salad bowl cannot withstand cleaning with a detergent and lukewarm water, best turn it in for a new salad bowl.

On Salad Greens and Their Preparation

There is a notion rife in America that it is quite French and proper to tear salad greens with the fingers. This method is presumably all right, but much better to some minds is to cut the greens to the desired size, shape, or length with a sharp knife. Tearing greens, with the exception of iceberg lettuce, tends to bruise them.

Iceberg lettuce is by far the commonest, most durable salad green in America and it is also the least interesting. The best salad greens include home-grown garden salads; watercress, available in many a mountain stream and riverbed; limestone or Bibb, Romaine, or Boston lettuce; snow-white endive, most of which is imported from Belgium; escarole, and curly endive or chicory.

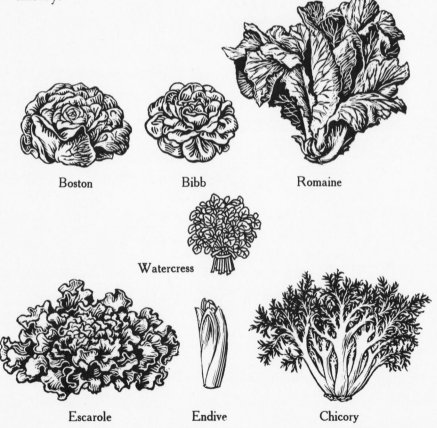

Boston   Bibb   Romaine

Watercress

Escarole   Endive   Chicory

Most salad greens should be rinsed in cold water after they are prepared for the salad bowl, then shaken or blotted with paper toweling to remove excess moisture. An inexpensive wire salad basket is ideal for shaking moisture out of wet salad greens. Prepared salad greens may be wrapped in plastic and chilled to crisp them for ½ hour or so before using.

Other Accompaniments

HOW TO COOK SPAGHETTI

The cooking of spaghetti is simplicity itself although there are apparently two common yet easily avoidable pitfalls that befall some cooks. The first is having the strands of spaghetti stick together; the other is overcooking.

The kettle in which the spaghetti is cooked should have at least a four-quart capacity.

One pound of spaghetti, the contents of one package, should be cooked in at least 3 quarts of water. A two-pronged fork should be on hand for immersing the spaghetti when it is added to the water. Here is how to cook perfect spaghetti.

1. Bring at least 3 quarts of water to a roaring boil. Add 1½ tablespoons salt.

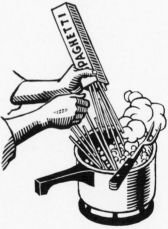

2. Add 1 pound of spaghetti (or less, if desired) while the water is boiling. Using a two-pronged fork, immediately start folding the spaghetti from the bottom to immerse it as quickly as possible in the water. The water must continue to boil constantly and the more rapidly the

better. Stir the spaghetti with the fork until all strands are bubbling free.

3. The cooking time for spaghetti varies from brand to brand and depends also on the size spaghetti. No. 9 spaghetti, called spaghettini, cooks in approximately 8 or 9 minutes. Thicker spaghetti takes longer. To test for doneness, lift a strand of spaghetti from the boiling water and bite into it. It should be tender but with a slight resilience or, as the Italians say, *al dente*. Of course, if you like spaghetti well done, by all means cook it until soft.

4. When the spaghetti is done, immediately add 1 cup of cold water to the kettle. This will stop the cooking without chilling the spaghetti.

Immediately empty the spaghetti into a colander to drain.

5. Have a hot platter ready with 2 to 4 tablespoons of butter in it.

Add the spaghetti and toss. Serve immediately with any of the tomato sauces outlined in this book plus their variations.

Of course, a good-quality spaghetti is excellent with only butter and Parmesan cheese.

Yield: Four to six servings.

LASAGNE

3 tablespoons peanut or
    olive oil
2 onions, finely chopped
    (about 1½ cups)
1 clove garlic, finely
    minced
1 pound round steak or
    chuck steak, ground
Salt and freshly ground
    black pepper to taste

3 cups fresh tomato sauce
    (*see page 95*)
6 quarts (24 cups) cold
    water
1 pound lasagne noodles
1 pound mozzarella cheese
1 pound ricotta cheese
½ cup grated Parmesan
    cheese

1. Preheat the oven to 350 degrees. Have ready a baking dish. Various sizes of baking dishes may be used to make lasagne, but one that measures 8 by 12 inches is a good size.

2. Heat 2 tablespoons of the oil in a skillet and add the onion and garlic. Cook until the onion is wilted and add the meat. Cook, breaking up the lumps in the meat with the side of a metal kitchen spoon. Cook and stir until the meat loses its red color. Add salt and pepper and tomato sauce. Bring to a boil and simmer for 20 minutes.

3. Meanwhile, pour the 6 quarts of water into a large kettle and add 3 tablespoons of salt, and the remaining tablespoon of oil. When it is boiling rapidly, add the lasagne noodles and cook until softened. Stir it around continuously with a wooden spoon so that it does not stick to itself or the bottom of the kettle. When the water starts to

boil violently again, let the lasagne cook for from 12 to 15 minutes, or until it is done. Do not overcook it. Remember that the lasagne will cook further when it is baked in the oven.

4. Spoon a thin layer of the meat sauce over the bottom of the baking dish and arrange a flat layer of the lasagne noodles over it. Spoon a layer of meat sauce over the lasagne. Cut the mozzarella cheese into thin slices and arrange one layer of mozzarella over the meat sauce. Spoon some ricotta cheese over this and a little Parmesan cheese. Add another

layer of noodles, more meat sauce, mozzarella, ricotta, and Parmesan. Continue making layers, ending with meat sauce and Parmesan. Up to this point the lasagne may be made in advance and refrigerated.

5. When ready to cook, place the lasagne in the oven and bake 20 minutes or longer, or until it is piping hot throughout and bubbling. Serve, if desired, with additional grated Parmesan cheese.

Yield: Six servings.

How to Cook Rice

Rice, the classic and delectable accompaniment for main courses, is one of the easiest dishes to prepare, and the mystery is why so many people regard cooking it as a chore. Rice may be cooked with water and salt or it may be given more body and substance by cooking it in various broths, such as chicken or beef. Rice is enhanced by such additions as onion, bay leaf, parsley, and mushrooms. Italians delight in rice with highly perfumed white truffles and a whisper of Parmesan cheese.

There are many kinds of rice in the world, but the three types grown in this country are the long grain, round grain or Japanese rice, and short grain. The best is the long grain, and the two best brands on the market are Uncle Ben's (the converted not the precooked) and Carolina rice. "Minute" rice is not worth the trouble it takes to cook it.

Remember that 1 cup of raw rice will produce about 4 cups cooked, the equivalent of four to six servings.

Three recipes for rice follow. The first is the simplest of all possible ways to cook rice and is useful for day-to-day cookery.

THE EASIEST RECIPE FOR RICE

2 cup water	1 cup rice
1 teaspoon salt	

Place the water in a saucepan and bring to a boil. Add the salt and rice and cover tightly. Reduce the heat and simmer gently for 20 to 25 minutes. At this point all the water should be absorbed and the rice tender.

Yield: Four to six servings.

PILAF OR PILAU

This recipe is elegant and although it takes a special effort it is altogether worth it.

2 tablespoons butter	2 cups fresh or canned
½ cup finely chopped onion	chicken broth
1 cup rice	

1. Heat the butter in a saucepan and cook the onion until it is wilted. Add the rice and cook, stirring, until golden. Do not brown.

2. Meanwhile, bring the chicken broth to a boil and add the broth to the rice, stirring. Cover tightly and simmer for 20 minutes.

Yield: Four to six servings.

THE BEST WAY TO MAKE RICE

This recipe is foolproof and yields a rice of uncommon delicacy with a buttery, rich flavor and every grain "standing apart," as some books put it. It is the method of Pierre Franey, one of America's greatest chefs.

2½ tablespoons butter	1½ cups fresh or canned
1½ tablespoons finely	chicken broth
chopped onion	½ bay leaf
1 cup long-grain rice	2 sprigs parsley
2 drops Tabasco sauce	Salt to taste, if necessary

1. Preheat the oven to 425 degrees.

2. Use a heavy ovenproof saucepan with a heavy lid (a lightweight saucepan will not work). Melt 2 tablespoons of the butter in the saucepan and add the onion. Cook, stirring, until onion is wilted but not brown.

3. Add the rice and cook, stirring, for about 30 seconds. Add the Tabasco sauce, chicken broth, bay leaf, parsley, and salt and bring to a boil. Cover and place the saucepan in the oven. Bake 20 minutes—no longer. The rice should now be done. When cooked all the water will be absorbed and the grains tender. If not, continue baking for 1 to 10 minutes longer. When done, dot with the remaining butter and toss lightly with a two-pronged fork.

Yield: Six to eight servings.

BAKING AND DESSERT-MAKING

*FROM MUFFINS TO POPOVERS, TO THE SIMPLE
ART OF BAKING BREAD, ROLLS, AND A DANISH . . .
A BASIC CAKE AND OLD-FASHIONED SUGAR COOKIES . . .
A FEW OF THE BEST-LOVED PIES . . . A DESSERT
SOUFFLÉ . . . THE ELEGANT CUSTARD DESSERTS
. . . FRUITS AND CHEESES*

Breads and Rolls

THERE ARE, basically, two kinds of breads, the quick breads and the yeast breads. The quick breads made with baking powder or soda are, as the name implies, mixed and baked in rapid succession. For the yeast breads it is necessary to allow the dough to rise before baking.

Recipes for both quick breads and yeast breads follow.

☞ Important Things to Know About Making Biscuits

Within limits, the amount of shortening used in making biscuits is not critical. For instance, in the following recipe the shortening may be increased to ½ cup. The result will be a richer biscuit.

Using the same recipe, cheese biscuits may be made by adding ½ cup grated sharp Cheddar cheese to the recipe just before adding the milk.

HOW TO MAKE BISCUITS

2 cups sifted flour   ⅓ cup shortening
1 teaspoon salt   ⅔ cup milk
2½ teaspoons baking
    powder

1. Preheat the oven to 425 degrees.
2. In a mixing bowl, combine the flour, salt, baking

powder, and shortening. Using a pastry blender, cut in the shortening until it has the consistency of coarse corn meal. Add the milk and toss gently with a two-pronged fork until all particles are moistened.

3. Gather the dough into a ball and turn it onto a lightly floured board. Knead the dough gently, about twelve strokes, with the heel of the hand. Gather into a ball once more. Lightly flour the board and roll the dough out with a lightly floured rolling pin to ½ inch thickness. Cut the dough into rounds with a floured biscuit cutter. Place the rounds on a baking sheet about ½ inch apart. Bake for 12 to 15 minutes.

Yield: About 16 two-inch biscuits.

☞ Important Things to Know About Making Muffins

Within limits, the amount of sugar used in making these muffins is not critical. The amount may be increased up to ½ cup for those who enjoy very sweet muffins.

Cheese muffins may be made by eliminating the sugar and adding ⅔ cup grated sharp Cheddar cheese before adding the milk and egg.

Nut muffins may be made by adding ½ cup chopped pecans or walnuts to the original recipe before adding the milk and egg.

HOW TO MAKE MUFFINS

2 cups sifted flour
1 teaspoon salt
1 tablespoon baking
    powder
2 tablespoons sugar

4 tablespoons (¼ cup)
    shortening
1 egg, lightly beaten
1 cup milk

1. Preheat the oven to 400 degrees.
2. In a mixing bowl, combine the flour, salt, baking powder, sugar, and shortening. Using a pastry blender, cut in the shortening until it has the consistency of coarse corn meal. Stir the egg into the milk and add it to he flour mixture. Stir just enough to moisten the dry ingredients to produce a lumpy batter.
3. Rub a dozen muffin cups with shortening and fill each two thirds full. Bake for 20 to 25 minutes.

Yield: 12 muffins.

THE BEST POPOVERS

Popovers, those crisp, gossamer, air-filled breads, are the American version of Yorkshire pudding. They are extraordinarily easy to make, as this recipe will testify.

1 cup flour
¼ teaspoon salt
2 eggs, lightly beaten

1 cup milk
1 teaspoon melted butter

1. Do not preheat the oven.
2. Sift the flour with the salt into a mixing bowl.
3. Using another mixing bowl, combine the eggs, milk, and melted butter. Beat lightly and stir the mixture into the flour. Stir until well blended and smooth.
4. Lightly oil the insides of 8 to 10 ovenproof glass custard cups. Fill the cups a little more than half full. Place the cups on a baking sheet and place in the oven. Immediately heat the oven. If an electric oven is used, heat it to 425 degrees; if a gas oven is used, heat it to 400 degrees. Bake the popovers in an electric oven for 1 hour; in a gas oven for 50 minutes.

Yield: 8 to 10 popovers.

Tips on Baking with Yeast

In all of cooking there is nothing perhaps more gratifying than the making of pastries in general and the baking of yeast breads in particular. There is something soul-satisfying in producing a loaf of bread, from the kneading of the dough to removing it from the oven.

And yet it is quite simple. But spend a moment or two to read the following.

1. When you work with yeast, you must take care that it is not dissolved in a liquid that is too hot. This will kill the thing that makes the dough rise. Water is the best liquid for dissolving yeast.

2. The proper temperature of water for dissolving yeast is from between 110 to 115 degrees. This is warmer than lukewarm but not hot. There are thermometers available in hardware stores for measuring such liquids but good judgment is just as good.

3. Before you start mixing ingredients, you should rinse the mixing bowl with hot water. This will help maintain the temperature which helps the yeast rise.

4. When the dough is added to the bowl it should be kept in a warm place free from currents of air. The simplest way to do this is to place the bowl containing the dough over a bowl of hot but not boiling water, then to cover the dough totally with a towel. The water below must be changed at intervals so that it stays hot.

5. The easiest method to determine when the dough has risen sufficiently is to press a couple of fingers into the dough ½ inch or so. If the impressions remain in the dough, it has risen enough. This is "double in bulk."

6. The best pans for baking bread are those made of glass

or of anodized aluminum. The latter has a dull finish. These absorb heat and give a good brown crust.

How to Knead Dough

When dough is turned out onto a table or board to be kneaded, shape it into a ball. Use the heels of the hands and push down heavily on the ball, pushing the dough away from

you. Give the dough a quarter turn and fold the upper half over toward you. Push down again as before with the heels of the hands. Give the dough another quarter turn and fold the upper half over as before. Keep up this motion, kneading repeatedly until the dough is springy and elastic. It may require a hundred kneading turns or more. But it's fun.

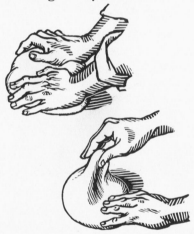

How to Punch Dough Down

To punch dough down, as recipes say, sink a fist in to the center of the swollen mass. As the dough collapses, pull the edges of the dough from the sides of bowl toward the center. Now, turn the dough upside down in the bowl.

HOW TO MAKE TWO LOAVES OF BREAD

1¾ cups milk
1 package dry yeast
½ cup warm water
2½ tablespoons sugar
1 tablespoon salt

2 tablespoons solid
    shortening, at room
    temperature
7 to 8 cups all-purpose
    flour

1. Note well that this recipe makes two loaves of white bread. Thus you will need two loaf pans, each measuring 9-by-5-by-3 inches.

2. Bring the milk just to a boil then set it aside. Let stand until milk is warm but not hot. Now start the recipe.

3. Rinse out a mixing bowl with hot water and dry well. Add the yeast and the ½ cup of warm water and stir to dissolve. Add the sugar, salt, and shortening and beat with a wooden spoon or an electric beater until the mixture falls from the beater in "sheets."

4. Add 4 cups of the flour while working the dough vigorously with your hands and fingers. This should require about 1 minute. Now add more flour, about ½ cup at a time, while working the dough. Add just enough flour so that the dough will stand clear of the bowl and not stick to the fingers.

5. Lightly flour a bread board and turn the dough out onto it. Wash out the mixing bowl and dry it thoroughly. Grease the bowl copiously with butter or shortening.

6. Knead the dough. Fold the dough over onto itself but toward you. Using the heel of both hands, push the dough down and away from you. Fold it toward you again and give the dough a quarter turn. Keep kneading the dough in this fashion until it is springy, elastic, and blistered. This should take about 10 minutes. Be sure to keep the board lightly floured so that the dough does not stick.

7. Place the dough in the prepared bowl. Turn the

dough around in the bowl so that the dough is greased all over. Cover loosely with a large, clean cotton towel. Place the bowl in a warm (about 80 to 85 degrees), draft-free place or preferably over a larger bowl of hot water. Let stand until "double in bulk," 1 to 2 hours. To test for "double in bulk," press two fingers lightly into the dough. If the imprints remain it is ready.

8. Punch the dough down. To do this, sink a fist into the center of the dough. Pull in the edges with your fingers and then turn the dough upside down in the bowl. Cover again and let the dough rise once more. This will take about 45 to 60 minutes.

9. Punch the dough down again and divide it approximately in half. Let the two portions rest while preparing the loaf pans.

10. Grease the inside of each of the loaf pans mentioned in step 1.

11. Start shaping the dough for the pans. To do this, take one portion of dough and pull it into a strip about twice the length of one pan. Bring the two ends of the dough together, slightly overlapping. Seal the edges by pinching with the fingers. Place the dough, seam-side down, in one of the prepared pans. Do the same with the other dough. Rub the top of each loaf with butter or shortening and cover lightly with kitchen towels. Let the dough rise until double in bulk, 50 minutes to 1 hour. The loaves will be ready for the oven if, when you touch them, a slight dent remains.

12. Meanwhile, preheat the oven to 425 degrees.

13. Place the loaves in the center of the oven and bake for 25 to 30 minutes or until perfectly brown. Immediately remove the loaves from the pans and place on racks to cool. Before cooling, brush the tops with melted butter. Like all breads, these loaves freeze well.

Yield: 2 loaves.

HOW TO MAKE YEAST ROLLS

1 package dry yeast	4 tablespoons (¼ cup)
¼ cup lukewarm water	shortening
1 teaspoon salt	½ cup milk
2 tablespoons sugar	2 to 2½ cups flour
	1 egg

1. Combine the yeast and water and let stand for 5 minutes. Stir to blend.

2. Combine the salt, sugar, and shortening in a mixing bowl. Bring the milk almost to a boil and add to the bowl, stirring. Mash the shortening against the sides of the bowl until shortening is broken into small lumps.

3. Stir in 1 cup of the flour and beat vigorously with a wooden spoon until the mixture is thoroughly smooth and elastic. Add the yeast and water mixture and the egg and stir until well blended. Stir in ¾ to 1 cup more flour. With floured fingers, add enough more flour to make a soft dough that does not stick to the fingers. Turn the dough onto a lightly floured board and knead for about 12 minutes, giving in all about a hundred kneading strokes.

4. Rub a large bowl with butter or shortening. Shape the dough into a ball and place it in the bowl. Rub the surface of the dough lightly with butter or shortening and cover the bowl with a light kitchen towel. Let the dough stand in a warm, draft-free place until double in bulk, 1 to 1½ hours. As noted earlier, the simplest method to keep the dough warm is to place the bowl over a larger bowl filled with hot but not boiling water. The water below must be changed at intervals so that it stays hot.

5. Punch the dough down by plunging a fist into the center and pulling the dough away from the sides of the bowl. Turn the dough once more onto a lightly floured

board. Roll the dough out and cut it into rounds with a floured biscuit cutter. Make a deep crease across the top of each roll with the floured handle of a knife. Fold the rolls over and gently press the edges together. Arrange the rolls symmetrically 1 inch apart on a greased pan. Cover with a light kitchen towel and let rise in a warm place for about 35 minutes.

6. Meanwhile, preheat the oven to 425 degrees.

7. Bake the rolls for 15 to 20 minutes or until golden-brown.

Yield: About 2 dozen.

DANISH COFFEE RING (A Rich Danish Pastry)

Would you believe that you can make Danish pastry of an excellence equal to the famed *Wienerbrød* of Copenhagen and infinitely better than that commonly found in the United States? With this authentic Danish recipe, it is easier than making pie.

3 to 4 cups flour
½ cup sugar
1 teaspoon salt
8 tablespoons (½ cup; 1
   stick) butter
¼ cup milk
1 package dry yeast

1 cup heavy cream
3 egg yolks (save whites for
   another purpose)
1 whole egg
2 tablespoons coarsely
   chopped unsalted nuts
   (pecans, walnuts, or
   blanched almonds)

1. Place a flour sifter inside a large mixing bowl and add 3 cups of flour, ¼ cup of the sugar, and the salt. Sift the mixture into the mixing bowl. Add the remaining flour *to the sifter* and set it aside, perhaps on a sheet of waxed paper.

2. Add the butter to the mixing bowl. Work the butter

with a pastry blender or quickly with the fingers until the mixture has the feel or look of coarse corn meal.

3. Heat the milk in a saucepan but do not let it boil; do not even let it simmer. The milk should be just a little warmer than lukewarm. (If a few drops of the milk are applied to the inside of the wrist they will feel warm but not hot.) Take the saucepan away from the heat and stir in 2 tablespoons of the remaining sugar and the yeast. Stir until the yeast and sugar are dissolved. Add the cream.

4. Place the 3 egg yolks in a mixing bowl. Beat with a wire whisk until light and lemon-colored. Stir the yolks into the cream mixture.

5. Pour the liquid into the flour mixture and stir. Mix all together with the fingers and hands. If the mixture seems too sticky, sift in more flour, a little at a time, until the mixture forms a soft dough. Shape the dough into a ball.

6. Rub a mixing bowl with oil or butter and add the ball of dough. Cover and refrigerate overnight.

7. In the morning, take the dough from the refrigerator and let dough stand for 20 minutes. Using a knife, cut the dough in half. With the hands, squeeze, press, and with a floured rolling pin, roll half of the dough into a long strip. Repeat this with the other half of the dough. Twist the strips around each other and make a circle by bringing the ends together. Brush the ends with a

little water and neatly press together to join them.

8. Oil or butter a baking sheet lightly and place the ring of dough on it.

9. Let the ring stand at room temperature for about 45 minutes or until it is double in bulk.

10. Preheat the oven to 350 degrees.

11. Beat the whole egg lightly and, using a pastry brush, brush the pastry ring with the egg. Sprinkle the ring with the remaining sugar and the chopped nuts.

12. Place the ring in the oven and bake for 35 to 40 minutes or until golden-brown and cooked through. Let cool almost to room temperature before serving. Serve, if desired, with butter and marmalade or other jellies and preserves.

Yield: Six to eight servings.

IF YOU DON'T MAKE YOUR OWN—HOW TO SERVE LONG LOAVES OF STORE-BOUGHT BREAD

Long loaves of French and Italian bread in America are always improved if before serving they are baked in a hot oven until they almost start to toast. This makes the crust crisper and tastier. It is simple to do. Simply preheat the oven to 450 degrees and when it is hot, place the bread on a rack in the oven. Let stand until crust starts to become browner, 5 to 10 minutes. Serve sliced, with butter.

HOW TO MAKE A DELICIOUS HERB BREAD WITH A LONG CRUSTY LOAF

1 long loaf of crusty
   French or Italian bread
4 scallions (green onions)

¼ cup finely chopped
   parsley
4 tablespoons (½ stick)
   butter

1. Preheat the oven to 400 degrees.

2. Place the long loaf of bread on a flat surface. Using a sharp knife, slice the bread lengthwise, end to end. Do not slice all the way through, however. The slicing will permit opening up the loaf like a sandwich while leaving one side as a "hinge."

3. Trim off the ends of the scallions. Rinse the scallions and dry them. Chop them finely with a sharp knife. Combine them with the chopped parsley.

4. Melt the butter in a saucepan. Stir in the herbs. Open up the loaf of bread and spoon the herb butter inside from one end to the other. Wrap the loaf in heavy-duty aluminum foil and bake for about 10 minutes. Cut the bread into 1-inch slices and serve piping hot.

Yield: Four to six servings.

Cakes and Cookies

A GOOD PLAIN YELLOW CAKE

2 cups sifted cake flour
1⅓ cups sugar
1 teaspoon salt
1 tablespoon double-acting
    baking powder

8 tablespoons (½ cup)
    solid, white vegetable
    shortening
1 cup milk
2 eggs
1 teaspoon vanilla extract

1. Place the oven rack just below the center of the oven.

2. Preheat the oven to 350 degrees.

3. Before you start to make the cake, do this: rub the inner bottoms of two 8-inch layer cake pans lightly with shortening. Using the fingers, sprinkle the inner bottoms and sides with flour, then hold the pans, one at a time, over the sink and shake out the excess flour.

4. To prepare the cake, combine the flour, sugar, salt, and baking powder in the bowl of an electric mixer and mix with a fork. Add the shortening and start beating on medium speed. Add ⅔ cup of milk and continue beating on medium speed for 2 minutes.

5. Add the eggs, remaining milk, and vanilla extract and beat for 2 minutes more.

6. Spoon half the batter into one of the prepared pans. Spoon the remaining batter into the other pan, using a rubber scraper to get most of the batter from the bowl.

7. Spread the batter neatly to the edges of the pans.

8. Place the pans on the oven rack, making certain they do not touch the back or sides of the oven.

9. Bake the cake for 30 to 35 minutes. To tell when the cake is done, at the end of 30 minutes' time, press the surface with the fingers, but very lightly. If the surface of the cake springs back, it is done. Otherwise the finger impressions will remain on the surface of the cake and you should continue baking for 5 minutes or more until it springs back when touched. When done, the cake will spring away from the sides of the pans.

10. Take the layers from the oven and place on a rack to cool. Let stand for 5 minutes and run a spatula around the sides of each pan. Place a cake rack over each layer and invert so that the cake comes out of the pan.

Yield: 2 layers.

SUGAR COOKIES

One of the easiest of dessert accompaniments is a simple sugar cookie. These cookies can be made in minutes and the dough lends itself to an amusing variety of shapes—that is, when the dough is rolled out, it may be cut into rounds, squares, diamonds, crescents, or whatever your fancy before baking. This recipe makes about 5 dozen cookies, but part of the dough may be frozen for later use.

8 tablespoons (½ cup) solid, white vegetable shortening	1 egg, lightly beaten
	⅓ cup milk
	1 teaspoon vanilla extract
1 cup sugar	2½ cups sifted flour

½ teaspoon cream of
tartar

½ teaspoon bicarbonate of
soda
¼ teaspoon salt

1. Preheat the oven to 400 degrees.

2. Sift together the flour, cream of tartar, soda, and salt. Set aside.

3. Combine the shortening, sugar, egg, milk, and vanilla extract in the bowl of an electric mixer. Start beating on low speed, then gradually increase the speed until the mixture is well blended. Reduce the beater's speed to medium and gradually add the flour mixture. Beat until thoroughly blended.

4. Lightly flour a board and place half the dough on the board. Roll the dough with a floured rolling pin until the dough is ⅛ inch thick. Cut the dough into any desired shape, such as rounds, squares, cresents, or diamonds. Place the cutouts on an ungreased baking sheet and bake for 5 to 7 minutes. Continue rolling, cutting, and baking the dough until all of it is used. Or, if you desire, you may wrap leftover dough in waxed paper or aluminum foil and freeze it for later use. If the dough is frozen it must be thawed before using.

Yield: About 5 dozen cookies.

Desserts

THERE ARE HARMONIES in the preparation of a meal just as there are harmonies in music. There should be a balance of flavors; dishes should complement each other; there should be a judicious use of salt and spices, oil and vinegar, and the textures of fish, meat, vegetables, or what-have-you should be various and in proper proportion. A perfect meal could not ignore dessert, whether it be a bowl of fruit, something baked, or something frozen. And the desserts should be chosen in accordance with what has gone before. The basic desserts are given here—pies, a dessert soufflé, custards, a mixture of fruits, and a delicate *crème brûlée*.

PIES

If ever a dessert has found universal favor in this country, it is a freshly made pie, whether it is a long fruit-filled tart from France or the traditional round, fluted-rim pie of America.

PIE PASTRY

1½ cups sifted all-purpose
flour
½ teaspoon salt

½ cup solid or nonliquid
shortening (this may be
part butter)
3 tablespoons water

1. Combine the flour and salt in a mixing bowl and add the shortening. Using a pastry blender, cut in the shortening until the mixture looks like coarse corn meal.

2. Sprinkle the mixture with water, a little at a time, while tossing and mixing the mixture with a two-pronged fork. When all the flour is lightly moistened, gather the dough into a ball. (The dough may now be rolled but it is better to wrap it in waxed paper and refrigerate, overnight if possible. Let the dough stand for 1 hour at room temperature before rolling.)

3. Flatten slightly the ball of pastry on a lightly floured board or pastry cloth. Using a rolling pin, roll the dough from the center outwards with short, quick strokes. Lift the rolling pin after each stroke. And, lift and turn the pastry occasionally to make sure it is not sticking to the board or cloth. Continue rolling to make a circle of dough ⅛ inch thick. Should the pastry tear—and ideally it shouldn't—patch it with a small scrap of dough. The circle of dough should be about 1½ inches larger in diameter than the pie plate.

4. Lift the dough onto the rolling pin and transfer it over a 9-inch pie plate. To do this, place the rolling pin close to the edge of the rolled-out circle of pastry. Carefully bring the pastry up against the sides of the pin and turn the rolling pin over and away from you while keeping the pastry close to the surface of the pin. When the pastry straddles the pin at the halfway mark it is ready to

transfer. Using a pair of kitchen scissors, neatly trim around the overhanging edge but leave a margin of 1 to 2 inches. Fold the overhanging pastry back and under itself. You may now flute the edge or you may crimp the rim of the pastry with the tines of a fork. To flute with the fingers, place the left forefinger against the inside of the pastry rim while pinching outside with the right thumb and forefinger.

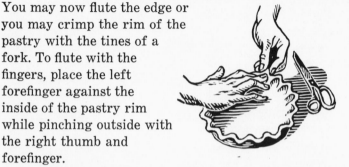

5. If the crust is to be filled before baking, do not prick the dough.

6. If the crust is to be baked before filling, there are two ways to go about it. One is to prick the bottom and sides of the dough generously with a fork and then bake in a pre-heated 425-degree oven for 12 to 15 minutes. Another method is to line the pastry with aluminum foil, then add enough raw rice or dried peas or beans to cover and weight the bottom. Then bake in a preheated oven for about 10 minutes. Remove the foil and rice or peas or beans and bake for 2 to 5 minutes more or until the crust is done. If the rim of the pastry starts to darken or burn, you should cover this part lightly with foil.

Yield: One 9-inch pie shell.

Of all pies, it is probably true that the two most popular are the cream pies and the berry or fruit pies. An example of each follows.

CHOCOLATE CREAM PIE

2 tablespoons flour
1½ tablespoons cornstarch
½ teaspoon salt
¾ cup sugar
2 cups milk
2 squares unsweetened
    chocolate
4 egg yolks, lightly beaten

(save whites for
    another purpose)
1 teaspoon vanilla extract,
    rum, or cognac
1 tablespoon butter
1 baked 9-inch pie shell
    (*see page 229*)
Sweetened whipped cream
    (*see recipe following*)

1. Combine the flour, cornstarch, salt, and sugar in a 1-quart saucepan. Using a wire whisk, stir in the milk, add the chocolate, and bring the mixture to the boil, stirring, over low heat. Cook, stirring, until chocolate melts and filling thickens.

2. Combine the yolks with a little of the hot filling, then return this mixture to the filling. Continue to cook, stirring, over very low heat for 2 minutes more. Remove from the heat. Add the flavoring and butter and let cool slightly. Pour into the baked pie shell and serve cold with sweetened whipped cream on top.

Yield: Six servings.

HOW TO WHIP CREAM

1 cup chilled heavy cream
2 tablespoons confectioners'
    sugar

¾ teaspoon vanilla extract

In warm weather particularly, it is important that the cream and mixing bowl for whipped cream be chilled. Add the cream to the mixing bowl and beat rapidly with a wire whisk, electric mixer, or rotary beater until mixture stands in peaks. Then beat in the sugar and vanilla. As the cream becomes increasingly frothy and thickened, lift the beater to test for thickness. The completed cream must be quite thick, but you must exercise caution. If you beat the cream too thoroughly for too long a time it will turn to butter.

Yield: 2 to 3 cups of whipped cream.

CHERRY PIE

1 unbaked 9-inch pie shell (*see page 229*)	1½ tablespoons tapioca
	¾ to 1 cup sugar
2½ cups canned red sour cherries, drained	¼ teaspoon salt
	½ teaspoon ground cardamom
1 cup juice from a can of cherries	1 tablespoon butter

1. Preheat the oven to 400 degrees.

2. When the shell is prepared, sprinkle over it the drained cherries.

3. Combine the juice with the tapioca, sugar, salt, and cardamom. Pour the mixture over the cherries and dot with butter. Bake for 30 to 40 minutes.

Yield: Six servings.

CREAM-CHEESE AND ALMOND PIE

Although the standard pastry I have given first is the most popular of all, there is much to recommend a graham-cracker crust. It is easier to make than the standard pastry, and here is an exceptionally tantalizing cream-cheese and almond pie using this simple and rather different-tasting crust.

½ cup blanched, toasted almonds (*see recipe following*)

1½ cups graham-cracker crumbs

4 tablespoons (½ stick) butter, melted

11 ounces cream cheese

¾ cup sugar

2 eggs, well beaten

½ teaspoon almond extract

2 cups (1 pint) sour cream

1. Preheat the oven to 350 degrees.

2. Whirl the nuts in an electric blender until they are pulverized, or otherwise grate them.

3. Mix the graham-cracker crumbs with the butter and press the crumbs over the bottom and sides of a 9-inch pie pan.

4. Blend the cheese with ½ cup of the sugar and the eggs. Beat until smooth and season with almond extract. Pour the mixture into the prepared crust and bake for 20 minutes.

5. Blend the sour cream with the remaining sugar and spread over the surface of the pie. Sprinkle with the grated almonds and return the pie to the oven for 3 minutes. Cool and chill.

Yield: Six servings.

How to Blanch Almonds

Drop shelled almonds with their light-brown coating into enough boiling water to cover. Simmer for 1 minute, then drain. Press the almonds between the fingers and the meat will slip out of the skin.

How to Toast Almonds

Preheat the oven to 350 degrees. Scatter blanched almonds over a baking sheet and bake, stirring frequently, until the almonds are golden and toasted, about 10 minutes. Let cool.

CHEESE PIE

This recipe is exceptionally easy to make and people dote on it. It is a pie but it tastes like cheesecake.

1½ cups graham-cracker
    crumbs
¾ cup plus 2 tablespoons
    sugar
4 tablespoons (½ stick)
    butter, melted
11 ounces cream cheese, at
    room temperature

2 eggs, well beaten
1 teaspoon vanilla extract
2 cups (1 pint) sour cream
2 cups sliced fruit
    (optional)
¼ cup confectioners'
    sugar (optional)

1. Preheat the oven to 350 degrees.
2. Combine the crumbs, 2 tablespoons sugar, and the butter. Using the fingers, press the crumbs against the bottom and sides of a 9-inch pie pan. This is the crust for the pie. Place it in the oven and bake for 5 minutes, no longer. Remove the crust-lined pan from the oven and let cool thoroughly.
3. Place the cream cheese into the bowl of an electric mixer and blend on low speed. Add half the beaten egg mixture and beat on low speed. When it is thoroughly blended, add the other half of the egg mixture and beat thoroughly.
4. Continue beating on low speed and gradually add ½

cup of the sugar and the vanilla extract. Pour the filling into the prepared crust, scraping the mixing bowl with a rubber spatula. Bake the pie for 20 minutes. Remove it from the oven.

5. Spoon the sour cream into a mixing bowl and stir in the remaining ¼ cup sugar. Stir and blend with a rubber spatula. Spoon this mixture on top of the pie and smooth the surface with the spatula.

6. Immediately turn the oven off. Put the pie back into the hot oven and let the pie remain there for exactly 4 minutes. Remove the pie from the oven and let cool. Put it in the refrigerator and chill thoroughly. When chilled the pie will set.

7. Combine the fruit and confectioners' sugar and serve with the pie. The sugared fruit is, as indicated, a matter of preference.

Yield: Six servings.

VANILLA SOUFFLÉ

3 tablespoons butter	1 tablespoon water
⅓ cup plus 1 tablespoon sugar	1 teaspoon vanilla extract
3 tablespoons flour	6 eggs
1 cup milk	1 cup heavy cream
⅛ teaspoon salt	4 tablespoons confectioners' sugar
2 teaspoons cornstarch	

1. Preheat the oven to 400 degrees.

2. Using the fingers, rub the inside of a 1½-quart soufflé dish with 1 tablespoon of the butter. Make certain the butter covers all the bottom and sides of the dish. Sprinkle the inside of the dish with 1 tablespoon of sugar and shake it around so that the sides are coated. Place the

dish briefly in the freezer, or refrigerate until ready to use.

3. Melt the remaining butter in a saucepan. Stir in the flour, using a wire whisk. When the mixture is blended, add the milk, stirring rapidly with the whisk. Bring the sauce to a boil, stirring constantly. When the mixture is thickened and smooth, add the remaining sugar and the salt. Continue cooking and stirring for about 1 minute.

4. In a small bowl, blend together the cornstarch and water and add to the sauce, stirring constantly. Continue cooking for about 1 minute. Remove the sauce from the heat and stir in the vanilla.

5. Break the eggs one at a time, letting the whites fall into a mixing bowl. Drop the yolks into another small mixing bowl. Beat the yolks lightly.

6. Using a rubber spatula, add the yolks to the sauce and beat rapidly with the whisk. Return the sauce to the heat and cook over very low heat, stirring. Let the sauce bubble, stirring constantly, for about 3 seconds, no longer.

7. Using a rubber spatula, transfer the sauce to a round-bottomed mixing bowl. Let the sauce cool for about 10 minutes at room temperature.

8. Beat the egg whites with a wire whisk, rotary beater, or electric mixer until they are quite stiff and stand in peaks. (It is all right to add the beaten egg whites to the sauce while the sauce is warm BUT NOT HOT.) Scoop half the beaten egg whites into the sauce and whisk them well into the sauce, using a rubber spatula or a wire whisk.

9. Scoop the remaining whites into the sauce. Using a cutting-in motion with a rubber spatula, cut down to the bottom, scoop around the bottom, and bring the spatula up. Do this several times. Do not overfold or the soufflé will not puff properly. Leave some white specks showing.

10. Using the spatula, pour the mixture into the pre-

pared soufflé dish. Place the soufflé in the oven and immediately turn the oven down to 375 degrees. Bake for 25 to 35 minutes. Some people like a soufflé with a moist interior, and for this the soufflé should be baked for the shorter period of time. For a soufflé with a firmer interior, use the longer cooking time.

11. Meanwhile, as the soufflé bakes, whip the cream (see page 231) and sweeten it with half the confectioners' sugar. Refrigerate until soufflé is cooked.

12. When the soufflé is removed from the oven, sprinkle it quickly with the remaining confectioners' sugar. The best way to do this is to hold a small sieve over the soufflé and to put the sugar in it. Shake the sieve this way and that over the soufflé until the top is coated. Serve the soufflé quickly with the whipped cream served on the side.

Yield: Four to six servings.

FRUIT MÉLANGE

This is a particularly good dessert to serve after a meal of several courses or a dinner with a heavy meat or casserole as the entrée. The variations on a fruit mélange are all but endless. The fruit mélange given here will serve four people and it may be varied according to season as the fruits come to market.

A fruit mélange should be served at the end of the meal.

2 cups ripe berries or fruit
  (*see note below*)
1 navel orange
4 dried figs
3 tablespoons confectioners'
  sugar

1 or 2 tablespoons spirits or
  liqueurs, such as rum,
  Kirsch, Cointreau, or
  Grand Marnier
  (optional)

1. If the berries or fruit have stems or if they need picking over, empty them into a colander in the sink. Pick over the berries or fruit and rinse under cold water as necessary. Drain well but do not dry. Pour the berries or fruit into a mixing bowl.

2. Peel the orange and pare away all the white skin. Carefully run the knife into the sections to cut them out. Add the sections to the berries or whatever.

3. Cut the dried figs into very thin strips, discarding the stems. Sprinkle with confectioners' sugar and refrigerate until ready to serve. If the spirits or liqueurs are to be used, add them at the last minute. Toss the berries, figs, and spirits together gently before serving.

Yield: Four servings.

NOTE: Compatible fruits for a mélange include seedless grapes, blueberries, strawberries, pitted black cherries, diced peeled pears, nectarines, cantaloupe balls, and watermelon balls.

ENGLISH CUSTARD

One of the best dessert sauces ever devised is what the French call a *crème anglaise* or English custard. It is smooth, rich and elegant, served hot or cold. It may be served over cake or ice cream or stewed fruit. There is only one trick in making this dish, and that is not to cook it over too high heat. The thing that thickens the custard are egg yolks, and if the heat is too high, these will "scramble," so to speak, and the sauce will curdle.

4 egg yolks (save whites for another purpose)
½ cup sugar
⅛ teaspoon salt

1¾ cups milk
½ teaspoon pure vanilla extract

1. Place an asbestos pad or a metal "Flame Tamer" on top of a burner; the pad or the Flame Tamer will distribute the heat from the burner more evenly

2. Place the yolks, sugar, and salt in a saucepan and stir with a wire whisk until well blended. Set this aside for a moment.

3. Pour the milk into another small saucepan and bring it almost but not quite to a boil. Add the milk, quite gradually, to the yolk mixture, stirring with the whisk. Immediately place the saucepan with the sauce over the pad and turn the heat to medium. Cook, stirring constantly with the wooden spoon. The important thing now is to keep the spoon in constant motion, going this way and that way, all over the bottom of the saucepan. Caution: the sauce must cook thoroughly until it is piping hot, but it must not boil. As the sauce cooks it will gradually thicken. There is one classic way to tell when the sauce is done. Lift the spoon from the sauce and hold it over the pan. Quickly run the forefinger down the center of the spoon. If the finger does not make a lasting impression on the sauce, it is not done. When the sauce is thick enough the finger will leave a definite clear space with the custard coating on either side.

4. Serve the custard hot or cold with cake slices, over ice cream, or over stewed fruit. Or use it to make a bavarian cream as in the following recipe.

Yield: Four to six servings.

ORANGE BAVARIAN CREAM

1 recipe for English
    custard, prepared
    according to the
    preceding recipe
¼ cup cold orange juice
1 envelope (1 tablespoon)
    unflavored gelatin

2 tablespoons orange-
    flavored liqueur such as
    Cointreau or Grand
    Marnier
1 cup heavy cream

1. Before you start making the English custard there are a few things to do in advance:

Place the orange juice in a small mixing bowl and set it aside.

Have the envelope of gelatin nearby and ready to add to the orange juice. Do not add it until the last minute, however, or it will harden as it stands.

Rinse out a 1-quart ring mold with cold water, empty it thoroughly but do not dry.

2. Prepare the English custard as indicated in the preceding recipe. As soon as it is done remove it from the heat.

3. Immediately empty the envelope of gelatin into the orange juice. Stir briefly with a rubber spatula. Let it stand a moment or two or until softened. When softened, scrape this into the hot custard with the spatula. Stir constantly until the gelatin is thoroughly dissolved and blended into the sauce. Pour the sauce into a mixing bowl. Stir in the orange-flavored liqueur and let the sauce cool almost to room temperature.

4. Whip the cream until stiff. Add a third of it to the sauce and fold it over and under with a rubber spatula into the cream, down, around, and up. Add another third of cream, incorporate it in the same manner, then the final third. When this has been lightly blended into the sauce,

pour the mixture into the rinsed-out mold. Carefully place the mold in the refrigerator and let stand for 4 hours or longer, or until the bavarian cream is thoroughly set.

Yield: Six servings.

CHERRY RUM SAUCE

This is an unusual, easily made and much talked about sauce for ice cream, cakes, and baked custards. It is made with cherry preserves, nuts, and dark rum. The rum must be dark because it imparts a flavor that white or light rum does not.

1 cup dark cherry preserves (preferably imported from England)	½ cup almonds, coarsely chopped pecans or walnuts ¼ cup dark rum

Combine all the ingredients and stir until blended. Spoon the sauce into a screw-top jar and cover closely. Refrigerate until ready to use. Serve spooned onto ice cream, cakes, and baked custards.

Yield: About 1¾ cups.

CRÈME BRÛLÉE

One of the most universally admired desserts in the world is the *crème brûlée,* or "burnt cream," of French cooking. It is unbelievably easy to make, and this is the simplest of recipes.

3 cups heavy cream

6 tablespoons granulated sugar

6 egg yolks (save the whites for some other use)

2 teaspoons vanilla extract

½ cup golden light-brown sugar

1. Preheat the oven to 300 degrees.

2. Pour the cream into a heavy saucepan and place it over low heat, preferably on an asbestos pad or "Flame Tamer." Add the granulated sugar and heat, stirring constantly, until the sugar dissolves and the cream is quite hot. Do not boil.

3. Place the yolks in a mixing bowl and beat them with a wire whisk, electric beater, or rotary beater until they are light in color. Gradually add the hot cream while stirring but not beating with the whisk. Stir in the vanilla extract.

4. Place a strainer over a 1-quart baking dish (a 1-quart soufflé dish may be used) and strain the cream mixture into the dish. Set the baking dish in another pan into which pour one inch of hot water; do it very gradually to prevent spilling. Carefully place the pan and baking dish in the oven and bake for about one hour or until a silver knife inserted in the center of the custard comes out clean. Do not overbake. Remove the custard from the oven and let stand at room temperature until cool. Place the custard in the refrigerator and chill thoroughly.

5. Just before serving, sprinkle the brown sugar over the surface of the custard. Set the baking dish on a bed of cracked ice and place it under a heated broiler. Do this quickly and remove the dish from the broiler as soon as the sugar is brown and melted. Serve immediately or chill it again and serve cold.

Yield: Six servings.

STRAWBERRIES WITH RASPBERRY PURÉE

One of the simplest conceivable desserts is fresh strawberries with a purée of raspberries. Defrosted raspberries put through a sieve or food mill work notably as a sauce.

2 ten-ounce packages
    frozen raspberries
2 pints (4 cups) fresh
    strawberries
	¼ cup confectioners' sugar
	2 or 3 tablespoons liqueur
	    (optional)

1. Defrost the raspberries according to the directions on the package. Press the raspberries through a sieve or put them through a food mill. The point is to eliminate as many of the seeds as possible. Discard the seeds and refrigerate the sauce until ready to serve.

2. Empty the strawberries into a colander and sit the colander in the kitchen sink. Rinse the berries under cold running water. Use a paring knife to remove the stems from the berries. Place the still-wet berries in a mixing bowl and sprinkle with confectioners' sugar. Refrigerate until ready to serve.

3. When ready to serve, place the berries in a dessert bowl and pour the raspberry purée over them. If desired, 2 or 3 tablespoons of liqueur may be added to the raspberry sauce. Suitable liqueurs would include Cointreau or Grand Marnier, Kirschwasser, or cognac.

Yield: Six servings.

FRUIT WITH CHEESE

The easiest of all meal-endings perhaps is fruit with cheese and this, too, is in the best of taste. Fruit with cheese is generally served when there is no other dessert.

The fruits may include pears (there is a time-worn admonition in Italy that "you should never tell the peasant how good pears are with cheese or he'll rob you out of both"), apples, grapes, oranges, peaches, black cherries, and so on.

The cheeses may include soft running cheeses, such as Brie, Camembert, Boursin, and Crèma Danica; soft but firm cheeses, such as Port du Salut, fontina, Muenster, Gruyère, Appenzell, and Danish esrom; and the blue cheeses.

The cheeses are preferably served with a long, crusty loaf of French or Italian bread, although many people enjoy English water biscuits or assorted crackers. It is traditional in France to serve cheese with pats of butter.

APPENDICES

A Glossary . . . Rules about Setting a Table . . . On Freezing Foods . . . On Making Coffee and Tea

Glossary

Al dente. An Italian term most frequently applied to the cooking of pasta such as spaghetti, macaroni, or noodles. It means that the dish in question should be cooked until done but not soft—that is to say, the food, when drained, should have some "bite" or resiliency when chewed. Other dishes that are frequently cooked *al dente* include rice and certain vegetables.

Aspic. A preparation made with a liquid to which gelatin has been added. Clear aspics are frequently used to coat such dishes as cold poached fish, meat, or poultry. There are also cold tomato aspics with vegetables, fish, or other foods; cold seafood aspics, and so on.

Beurre Manié: see Roux

Bind. To use a sauce, such as mayonnaise or cream sauce, to hold other ingredients together. For example, if you are making a tuna salad containing chopped celery, onions, green pepper, and so on, these will be "bound" together with mayonnaise.

Blend. To mix various ingredients together in a uniform manner. For example, one blends flour and butter with a whisk or beater before adding milk or another liquid to make a sauce. When the liquid is added, it, too, is stirred and cooked until blended and smooth. One of the best and most practical utensils for blending is the electric blender, although the action of the blender does far more than blend soups, sauces, vegetables, and on on. It is also excellent for "grating" such things as bread and cheese.

Brown. There are many ways to brown dishes. Meats, vegetables, poultry, and so on are frequently browned by cooking on both sides in hot fat. Various other methods of browning include placing foods in hot ovens, under broilers, and on top of hot gas or charcoal-fired grills.

Coat. Foods are frequently coated with flour, bread crumbs, cracker crumbs, and sometimes grated nuts before they are cooked. Flour helps the meats and other foods to brown more quickly and also tends to seal in flavors.

Croûtons. Small cubes or very thin slices of bread that have been lightly toasted or cooked in oil or butter until golden-brown and crisp.

Curdling. The breaking down of a sauce or other liquid so that it is no longer one smooth, homogenous mass. Curdling will occur, for example, if the heat is too high when egg yolks are stirred into a sauce, because the egg in effect goes beyond the thickening point and cooks as though it is scrambled. If too much oil is added to yolks while making mayonnaise, or if the oil is added too rapidly in the beginning, the mayonnaise will curdle.

Drippings or **pan drippings.** This is the fat or liquid that comes from poultry or meat when they are roasted, grilled, sautéed, or fried. It is, in other words, all the natural liquids surrounding foods when they are cooked in a skillet or roasting pan. It would not apply, of course, to the water in which vegetables are simmered.

Dust. This term is most commonly used in the expression "dust lightly with flour." It means to dip the foods in flour so that the flour will adhere lightly.

Entrée. In America the entrée means the main dish of the meal. In French menu planning it has several more involved meanings, but it is generally the third course of a meal.

Flute. In pastry making this term applies mostly to the making of pies. The rims of pies are fluted by turning the outer rim of a pie shell over or under itself, building up the rim with the fingers, and making a pattern, generally "flowing" or wavy. To flute the edge or rim of a pie is to make this pattern.

Garnish. To add something to a dish as a final decorating touch. The choice is practically without limit. The garnish could be a sprig of herb such as parsley or rosemary, a radish rose, quartered hard-cooked eggs, tomato wedges, or, for the most elegant dishes, cutouts of baked pastry such as those in the shape of crescents.

Gelatin. Gelatin can be a natural agent or a powder. All fresh bones of meat, fish, or poultry contain some natural gelatin that is released when cooked in a liquid, be it water, soup, or stew, and that is what causes some soups and stews to become firm and "jelly-like" when they are cold. Most often in the home, however, gelatin is a powder that is first softened in a little liquid. After the gelatin is softened, it is then added to a hot liquid such as a fish, chicken, or meat broth or hot seasoned liquid like tomato juice. Various foods, such as crab meat, lobster, shrimp, vegetables, and so on, can be added to any of those liquids and then the liquid will become firm when it is chilled. Some gelatin dishes are sweet and are used for desserts, some are savory and serve as salads, first courses, or luncheon dishes. Almost all savory gelatin desserts are called aspics (q.v.).

Glaze. To glaze is to cause a golden-brown layer to form on certain dishes by running them under a broiler or other source of heat. Glazing also occurs when many dishes—macaroni in cream sauce, for example—are baked in the oven.

Hors d'oeuvre. A French term meaning appetizer. In English the plural of the word is almost always spelled "hors d'oeuvres," that is to say with an "s" at the end. Properly speaking, however, the plural is "hors d'oeuvre" without the final "s" in French.

Lard: To lard is to put ribbons of fat into various meats, using a small sharp knife or using a special instrument called a larding needle. In most cases it is preferable to have a butcher perform the larding.

Purée. This is to put solid foods such as potatoes, carrots, green beans, and broccoli through a food mill, masher, or ricer. The commonest purée in America is probably mashed potatoes. Most baby foods that aren't solids are purées.

Render. This is to cook foods in a skillet or other utensil so that they give up their fat. Each time that bacon is cooked in a skillet, for example, it is rendered of its fat.

Roux. This is a blend of butter and flour, the basis for countless thousands of sauces. The butter and flour are generally cooked together briefly before a liquid is added, which in turn becomes thickened and smooth to produce a sauce. A *roux* of butter and flour, worked together until smooth, is called a *beurre manié* and may be added to boiling sauces, bit by bit, to thicken the sauces.

Sauté. In France the word *sauter* means, literally, "to jump." With reference to cuisine, it means cooking small portions of meats, poultry, fish, or vegetables in a small amount of fat until done. It is a form of frying, but the term "frying" generally means to cook in a larger quantity of fat.

Sear. To sear is to cook meats or poultry on all sides until quite brown, generally over quite high heat. In theory the "searing" helps seal in the juices of the meat so that less juice will flow from the meat while cooking.

Shred. To cut or pull apart a food—a vegetable or a cooked meat, for instance—into thin strands or slivers. Carrots, potatoes, and the like are usually shredded with a knife or cutter; well-done meats such as a long-simmered pot roast can be shredded with the fingers.

Sliver. To cut or chop a food such as almonds into thin bits or strips.

Steam. To cook such foods as lobsters, cauliflower, artichokes, and so on in a utensil that is placed over boiling water. The bottom of the utensil must not touch the boiling water and it must be tightly closed. The foods are cooked by the high temperature of the steam given off by the water.

Truss. To tie poultry, fish, or whatever with string and/or skewers so that it will not lose its shape while cooking.

Whip. To beat with a wire whisk or other beater such foods as cream and egg whites, mashed potatoes, and sauces. Whipping causes cream and egg whites to mound in volume as air is beaten in. Mashed potatoes become lighter. Sauces may be whipped to make them lighter or to cool them off.

Yeast. A leavening agent that causes breads and other pastries to rise when they sit at a certain temperature. Yeast is a natural, living organism that is activated by heat and causes fermentation.

On Setting a Table

Almost every authority who has written on the subject has different notions about setting a table. There is common agreement on one point, however: knives and spoons are generally placed to the right of the dinner or service plate, forks to the left. And the silver is arranged in accordance with the menu, in a pattern so that guests will pick up the utensils used first, working from the outside in.

Other than that there are not any rock-bound rules about table settings. Thus it is best to rely on your own logic. As an example, however, you may note the place setting that follows for a dinner consisting of soup, chicken sauté with noodles, salad with cheeses and bread, fruit, and wine. It is supposed that a white wine will be served with the chicken dish, a red wine with the cheeses. You never serve two different wines in the same glass.

Note that the soup spoon is on the outside since it will be used first. After the soup is disposed of, the two outside pieces become the dinner knife and the dinner fork to be used with the chicken dish. When that is disposed of, you are left with a salad fork to the left, a knife to the right, to be used with the cheese. When they are disposed of, you are left with the dessert fork and spoon arranged at the top of the dinner plate.

The use of a dessert fork and spoon is not as common in America as it is in France, but it is practical, the fork for pushing, the spoon for eating, and vice versa, depending on the dish: berries and cream desserts with a spoon, cake and pie with a fork.

The reason the dessert fork and spoon are placed above is simply because if they were placed to either side of the dinner plate with the other silver, it would look cluttered. It is not necessary, in fact, to place the dessert fork and spoon (or fork alone) when the table is set. They may be brought to the table just befor or simultaneously with the dessert.

The use of a service plate (a plate put in the center of each place setting before guests are seated) is not essential, but it has more style than place setting without. The service plate is generally removed after the soup course or appetizer if there is one. If there is no soup course or appetizer, the service place is removed before the main course is served.

First Course: Clear turtle soup
Main Course: Chicken sauté with noodles
Salad Course: With assorted cheeses and heated French bread
Dessert: Mélange of fruits
Coffee

This is the way one proposed place setting with wineglasses might look:

On Freezing Foods

═══════════════════

It has always been a mystery to me why books on freezing foods are written. The pages of most of them are padded with recipes which, as far as I can discern, have no marked virtues that make them eminently suited for cold storage. The fact is that the vast majority of all prepared dishes—casseroles, soups, sauces, stews, meat loaves, and so on—can be frozen to advantage.

Common sense should dictate foods that do not freeze well. These would include:

> Mayonnaise and dishes made with mayonnaise.
> Aspics and other dishes containing gelatin.
> Hard-cooked eggs.
> Custard pies.

Sauces such as hollandaise and *béarnaise* and other sauces thickened at the last minute with egg yolks may be frozen but this is not recommended. It requires an expert hand to reconstitute them without curdling.

With rare exceptions almost all *cooked* vegetables and vegetable casseroles freeze well. An exception would be boiled potatoes.

Very few *raw* vegetables and fruits freeze well but some of them may be frozen provided they are to be used later for cooking. This would apply to raw tomatoes, corn on the cob, and melon balls.

Almost all fresh herbs may be frozen, including tarragon, parsley, and thyme. To freeze them they should first be rinsed then wrapped tightly in plastic bags.

As a general rule it is best not to refreeze foods that have been completely defrosted. This is a cautionary measure, however. If the foods in question have been frozen and defrosted under the most sanitary, proper conditions, they would not be injurious if refrozen. Baked goods can always be defrosted and refrozen successfully.

No foods improve with long freezing and it is best to consume frozen foods within the shortest possible time after they are stored, within one or two months if possible. One year is recommended as the maximum time for holding any frozen food.

Freezing tends to diminish the strength of spices in various foods. Thus, when a frozen food is defrosted and reheated it is best to taste the food and season it once more to taste.

By all means, when freezing foods or liquids in glass jars or plastic containers, leave enough head space to allow for expansion once the food or liquid is frozen. For dry-pack foods such as cooked shrimp, ½ inch of head space would be sufficient. For liquid and semi-liquid foods, leave at least ½ inch for a pint container; at least 1 inch for quart containers.

The best freezer materials are those that are both moisture- and vapor-proof. These include aluminum foil, plastic wraps, plastic jars and cartons, and glass jars.

When wrapping foods that do not require head room in sheets of foil, plastic, and so forth, you should wrap as closely as possible to exclude as much air as possible. Air pockets can yield to rancidity.

Improperly wrapped foods, those stored in materials that are not moisture- and air-proof, will develop freezer-burn—grayish-white spots which spoil the texture of the foods when defrosted.

It is extremely important to label all foods carefully both with the name of the contents and with the date of freezing. Various kinds of adhesive tapes, labels, and markers are available for this purpose.

Eggs freeze well if they are to be used later for cooking. Whole raw eggs and raw egg yolks require a bit of special treatment for freezing. To prepare whole raw eggs for freezing, break the eggs into a bowl and stir lightly with a fork to blend whites and yolks. For every cup of whole eggs, stir in ½ teaspoon of salt. Pour them into a container and freeze.

To freeze only the yolks, first stir them lightly with a fork and for each cup of yolks add 1 teaspoon of salt. Press them through a mesh sieve into a container for freezing.

Egg whites do not require special treatment for freezing.

When the eggs are defrosted, you might follow this table of equivalents for measuring them:

> 3 tablespoons blended yolks with whites = 1 egg
> 2 tablespoons defrosted egg whites = 1 egg white
> 1½ tablespoons egg yolks = 1 egg yolk

Milk, cream, and butter freeze well. Make certain that there is head room in the plastic containers for milk and cream and they may be frozen directly in the carton. Butter may be frozen in the carton in which it is packaged. If the butter is to be stored for an extensive period, it is best to overwrap it in foil or other suitable freezer wrap.

Sour cream acquires a grainy texture when frozen, but, once defrosted, it may be whipped with a whisk until smooth.

If you are going to freeze noodle or spaghetti dishes, they should be slightly undercooked for best results because they will be reheated when defrosted.

On Making Coffee and Tea

There are some people who can make anything, including breathing, seem complicated. There are those who can make the simple act of preparing a cup of coffee or tea seem as intricate and involved as the making of a banquet. Actually the rules are few and, happily, variable. You might remember, however, that the taste of water varies from one community to another and this affects the flavor of coffee or tea. The purer the water the better the result.

HOW TO MAKE COFFEE

The most important thing in coffeemaking is the cleanliness of the pot. It should be scrubbed well after each use and washed with soap and water.

The recommended proportions for making coffee are ¾ cup water to 1 coffee measure.

This proportion applies whether the pot is drip, percolator, filter, or whatever. If on the other hand you find that the coffee thus produced is too weak for your taste, then by all means increase the quantity of coffee; or if it too strong, then reduce the quantity.

When the coffee is drunk, empty the pot, pour out the grinds, and wash the pot well. The grinds, incidentally, may in almost all circumstances be put down the drain of the kitchen sink. They will not clog it.

HOW TO MAKE TEA

Absolute cleanliness is not as essential in a teapot as it is in a coffeepot but the teapot, nonetheless, should be washed frequently and thoroughly after one or two uses. When you discard used tea leaves, empty them onto paper toweling or waxed paper, which may then be rolled into a ball for discarding.

The essential thing in making tea is that the water be brought to a furious boil. Purists will heat the teapot first by pouring some of the boiling water into the pot, letting it stand briefly before emptying. I find this unnecessary for all practical purposes and I simply put 1 teaspoon of tea (I measure this with my fingers) into a teapot and pour in 1 cup of the boiling water.

THE WONDERFUL WORLD OF TEAS— AN EXPLORATION

It is literally true that there is no soft beverage in the world more bracing than tea. And teas come in such fascinating varieties and blends they are a joy to explore. Generally speaking, there are three kinds of teas: the black, which is commonest;

the green, or "unfermented," teas; and the flowery or "perfumed," teas.

If you are starting a "sampler" of teas, there are three that may be recommended: darjeeling, Earl Grey, and lapsang souchong. These are mentioned because each has very special qualities that are evident at first sip.

Darjeeling has been called the prince of teas and the tea of princes. It is commonly said to have the finest and most delicate flavor of Indian teas. It has a pure, clean taste and is excellent either for breakfast or as something to awaken the senses.

Earl Grey is a blend of many teas and is produced by several tea concerns. No two formulas may be the same, and yet they are similar. Earl Grey could be called a "romantic" tea, and some blends taste vaguely of dried orange peel. It is an adventure.

Lapsang souchong is the best known of the "smoky" teas. It has an interesting, much-coveted smoky flavor.

As a fourth tea you might well discover, if you do not know them, the flowery teas available. The best known is jasmine, which actually does contain jasmine blossoms that are "reconstituted" when the tea is brewed.

As time goes by you might wish to sample the following black teas: Assam, Ceylon, English breakfast, and keemun (said to have a winy flavor).

The green teas, such as basket fired or gunpowder pearl, have a sharp, almost acrid taste and are frequently associated with Japan.

Among the oolong teas, Formosa oolong is best known. It is frequently said to taste of ripe peaches.

The method of brewing all these teas is the same.

Index

i

A Note About the Author

CRAIG CLAIBORNE was born in 1920 in Sunflower, Mississippi, and grew up in Indianola. He attended Mississippi State and was graduated with a degree in journalism from the University of Missouri.

For several years he worked in public relations in Chicago, then served in the Navy during the Korean War, and following his discharge enrolled in the Swiss Hotelkeepers' Association School in Lausanne, from which he eventually graduated eighth in a class of sixty. When he returned to the United States he worked for *Gourmet* magazine and for a public relations firm specializing in food accounts until 1957, when he was hired as Food Editor of *The New York Times*. In that position he has become a nationwide authority on food; he appears frequently in the magazine and television media and since 1961 he has produced three cookbooks and a New York restaurant guide.

A Note on the Type

THIS BOOK *was set on the Linotype in two type faces. The Caslon face, an artistic, easily read type, has had two centuries of ever-increasing popularity in our own country; it is of interest to note that the first copies of the Declaration of Independence and the first paper currency distributed to the citizens of the newborn nation were printed in this type face. The Century Expanded face, used for the recipes and special text portions of this book, was based on the Century type face designed by L. B. Benton in 1890 for the American Type Foundry. This face was especially cut for the printing of* Century *magazine, supplying a bolder and more readable letter-form than the thinner type faces in general use at the time.*

This book was composed and bound by The Haddon Craftsmen, Inc., Scranton, Pennsylvania, and printed by Universal Lithographers, Timonium, Maryland. The line illustrations were handsomely rendered, in the rarely used scratchboard technique, by Tom Funk. The typography, endpaper, and binding were designed by Kenneth Miyamoto.